A Breed
Apart

Nova Scotia's
Duck Tolling Retriever

Gail MacMillan

NIMBUS
PUBLISHING LTD

(Christopher Studios, Bathurst, N.B.)

This book is dedicated to the memory of our beloved Nova Scotia Duck Tolling Retriever, Harbourlights Highland Chance CD (April 15, 1991 - Sept. 20, 1997). Her life was like that of a rose in bloom, too brief but beautiful in every way.

Ron and Gail MacMillan, October 1997

Nimbus Publishing Limited
PO Box 9301, Station A
Halifax, NS   B3K 5N5
(902)455-4286

Design: Kate Westphal, Graphic Detail Inc., Charlottetown, PEI

Cover caption: (front) Harbourlights Highland Chance CD;
(back) Harbourlights Scotia Ceilidh. (Photos Ron MacMillan)

Title page caption: Dianne Crowell's dog JesSea.
(Courtesy Dianne Crowell)

Printed and bound in Hong Kong

Canadian Cataloguing in Publication Data
MacMillan, Gail.
 A breed apart
Includes bibliographical references.
ISBN 1-55109-231-X
1. Nova Scotia duck tolling retriever.   I. Title.
SF429.N68M33 1998   636.752'7   C98-950107-8

Nimbus Publishing acknowledges the financial support of the
Canada Council and the Canadian Department of Heritage.

Contents

Preface

This book's bibliography is not lengthy. And with good reason. Most of the material is original, related first-hand to the author for first-time recording. Therefore, compiling this manuscript was an absorbing and exciting task.

My enjoyment of the work came mostly from the people I met along the way. The residents of Yarmouth County and beyond who had been involved with Nova Scotia's tolling retrievers over the years were a delight to encounter and, without exception, among the most agreeable and generous individuals I have ever met. Some, like Laura Bradley, archivist at the Yarmouth County Museum and Historical Research Library, and Erna Nickerson of Harbourlights Kennel, I already regarded as good friends before the outset of the project. These two wonderful women uncompromisingly supported me again as they have so frequently in the past. I cannot thank them enough for their unrelenting assistance and sincere friendship.

Early in the project I was introduced to another generous Yarmouth woman. Joan Semple of Murray Manor is the daughter of legendary tolling retriever breeder and trainer Eddie Babine. Joan has been invaluable with her constant willingness to help in spite of an extremely busy lifestyle. A fax to Joan meant immediate attention to any problem I was experiencing.

The daughter of another major player in tolling retriever history also offered her unlimited assistance and proved to be a diligent researcher. Ann Colwell-Murdoch, daughter of Col. Cyril Colwell, rolled up her sleeves and went to work writing her memories of her father and searching out details and dates. She, like her brother John, who allowed access to Colonel Colwell's extensive files, has been a great supporter.

I also was privileged to meet the Armstrong family of Bellneck. What a delightful experience! Paul and Bernadette Armstrong gave freely of their time, photos, and memories. Their warmth and sense of humour never flagged. Bernadette even shared her recipe for one of her favourite traditional Acadian dishes, rappé pie.

Then came my two "super sleuths," Helen Matheson of Digby and Sam Rodgerson of the Melbourne Road, Yarmouth County. Helen travelled the roads of Yarmouth County, questioned residents, and trekked through kennels in her quest to help ferret out the truth about the tolling retrievers' roots. She also supplied many of the wonderful photos of Sheriff H. A. P. Smith (her step-grandfather) for this book.

And then there was Sam Rodgerson who, in spite of ill health, worked diligently to set me on the right path to the descendants of Eddie Kenney. Sam spared no effort in helping to fill in the gaps in the life story of this early breeder and shared his own memories of more than fifty years of hunting with tolling retrievers to boot.

As a result of Sam's detective work, I met Audrey Goudey, Eddie Kenney's granddaughter. Audrey was a wealth of information about this man so important in the dogs' development and history. Her love for her grandfather came through in every descriptive word and she, too, instantly became an excellent researcher in seeking out facts about Eddie and his dogs. She even found a new family mystery to explore.

Ann and Bruno Boudreau were other excellent sources of information. I am grateful to Ann for taking the time and expense to call and put me in contact with her Uncle Bruno, a tolling retriever expert of long standing.

Evelyn LeBlanc's letters, in response to my request for information on Nova Scotia's tolling retrievers in the Letters to the Editor section of the Yarmouth newspaper, touched me deeply with their heartfelt sincerity.

Another response to my letter came from Bill Crowell of Yarmouth. He put me in touch with Bill Sutherland whose father had been a friend of Col. Cyril Colwell. Their common bond was their interest in Nova Scotia's tolling retrievers. Bill recalled those days with warmth and vivid detail.

Linda Cann, editor of the *Acadia Bulletin*, also replied with an extensive file she has been putting together over the years on Nova Scotia Duck Tolling Retrievers.

Greg Bennet and Fred Hatfield of *The Yarmouth Vanguard* supported the project as well. Without the publication of my Letter to the Editor, much important information may well have been missed.

Helma Wood and Trudy Parker at the Admiral Digby Museum helped. They put me in touch with a descendant of H. A. P. Smith and pinpointed his various residences.

David Wood of Springhill generously shared his findings from years of investigating Toller history and pioneering with the dogs in the show ring. David's generosity, like that of his mentors, John and Mary Sproul, is a constant aspect of his character.

MLA Allister Surette responded with alacrity when asked to contribute the story of his bid to have the Nova Scotia Duck Tolling Retriever officially declared the province's official canine. Mr. Surette is adamant in his conviction that Nova Scotia Duck Tolling Retrievers should take their rightful place in the province's history and become a living part of its proud heritage.

Eldon Pace helped, too. But then, helping is a way of life for this amazing gentleman from Shubenacadie. Perhaps the only time Eldon isn't entirely cooperative is when he is asked to tell his own remarkable story. His innate modesty inhibits his telling about his many years of dedication to the province's official canine as well as to its wildlife.

Harbourlights Highland Chance CD poses for the camera. (Photo Ron MacMillan)

And then, of course, there is James C. Jeffery (Jim) with his keen insight not only into the tolling retriever breed but also into the people and history of "ducking" in Yarmouth County. Jim's analytical mind provided much "grist for the mill" when testing theories and getting a realistic overview of tolling retriever development in Yarmouth County. Jim was one of the very few far-sighted people who, in 1978, had the presence of mind to capture on audio tape, the stories and wisdom of some of the remarkable old "tolling" men of Yarmouth County. I am indebted to Jim for sharing his extensive knowledge gained through years of studying tolling retrievers.

Near the completion of my research I finally managed to contact Andy Wallace of Ireton, Yarmouth County. He has been breeding Little River Duck Dogs for thirty years and holds to the principles of legendary breed developers like Eddie Kenney and Eddie Babine.

Andy's dogs are hunters and companions, bred for their original purpose, not intended for the show ring or Canadian Kennel Club recognition. They are the grass roots tolling retrievers of Nova Scotia, and Andy Wallace is their devoted caregiver in the tradition of those breeders of a half century ago who loved their dogs and truly were a breed apart.

Introduction

Meet the Nova Scotia Duck Tolling Retriever

The ducks come toward the shore, drawn by a force as ageless as magnetism and just as powerful, to where a small red dog, its white-tipped tail flagging, cavorts about, careless of its mesmerizing effect on the birds.

When the curious flock is only a few yards from land, the dog vanishes into a tangle of brush and grass. Puzzled, the ducks pause. Where has that alluring creature gone, they seem to wonder. And then a human leaps up from the dog's hiding place. Startled, the birds burst into flight. A shotgun blasts and some of the flock have fallen victim to that amazing pied piper of the marsh, the Nova Scotia Duck Tolling Retriever.

For anyone unfamiliar with the dogs and their astonishing ability to lure waterfowl, this is an amazing scenario. In the 1960s these tolling retrievers were actually featured in Ripley's famous "Believe It Or Not" newspaper column syndicated throughout the United States and Canada.

Fame, however, came slowly to Nova Scotia's tolling retrievers (also known as Yarmouth Tollers, Little River Duck Dogs, Little Rivers, or simply Tollers). Although recognized as a distinct breed by the Canadian Kennel Club in 1945, they did not quickly capture the interest of dog fanciers beyond their native Yarmouth County.

For more than two hundred years the small amber canines had been largely unknown outside of southwestern Nova Scotia. Hunters and breeders in that area knew they had a good thing and felt no pressing need to share it with the rest of the world. These years in relative obscurity would later earn the little dogs the reputation of being Nova Scotia's best kept secret.

In 1980 the spotlight of the dog fancy world suddenly fell on two Nova Scotia Duck Tolling Retrievers. In June of that year, Sproul's Highland Playboy bred by John and Mary Sproul of Springhill, N.S., and owned by Linda Barnes took a Best In Show at a Canadian

This question seems to hang in the air as this Toller looks back: "Want me to go again?" (Photo Ron MacMillan)

Kennel Club sanctioned event in Saskatchewan; a few days later, White Ensign owned by Roy and Alison Strang of Surrey, B. C., captured a similar title at a British Columbia show. These events marked the beginning of a new era of recognition in Nova Scotia Duck Tolling Retriever history.

In 1988, in observance of the Canadian Kennel Club's one hundredth anniversary, Canada Post issued a thirty-seven-cent stamp bearing an artist's conception of the Nova Scotia Duck Tolling Retriever. Nine years later the Royal Canadian Mint put out a sterling silver fifty-cent piece with the dog's likeness emblazoned on it.

May 1995 brought the little red dogs a lasting place in the history of their native province. Largely through the efforts of Allister Surette, the MLA for Yarmouth, they were officially declared Canada's first and only provincial canine.

What is Tolling?

Tolling, in a hunting context, describes the process of luring game (usually waterfowl) with the use of small animals (usually dogs). This definition comes from one meaning of the verb "toll" which is to "attract, entice, alure." Tolling church bells, for example, draw or attract people to church.

The noun "toll" may play a more subtle role in the Nova Scotia Duck Tolling Retriever's breed name in the sense that a toll is something paid, lost, suffered. Certainly many waterfowl that have been drawn to the tolling retrievers of Nova Scotia have paid dearly.

The reason for this seemingly inane behaviour by usually canny birds is unknown. Is it mere curiosity that draws ducks (and sometimes geese) to their doom? Is it a defence strategy? Or is it the result of some strange phenomenon of nature, which will never be fully understood until someone deciphers the deductions of a duck? Whatever the explanation, the attraction has proven effective for hundreds of years.

People first realized the advantages of tolling for waterfowl when they witnessed its implementation by that wiliest of all marshland predators, the red fox. The fox would cavort about on the shore, its white-tipped tail flagging, in clear sight of ducks rafting far out on the water. The ducks, drawn by this display, would swim closer and closer until, *snap!* The fox's mate would leap from its hiding place in the tall weeds and grass and seize their dinner.

At other times a fox hunting alone would prance and jump about on the beach well within view of the ducks until the birds began to move shoreward. Then he would stretch out on his belly, hidden in the marsh grass, and wait.

Whenever the ducks hesitated on their shoreward journey, the fox had only to raise his white-crested tail and flick it to and fro a few times to start them moving again. Soon they were within range and shortly it was evident that even a bachelor fox could manage his own version of Peking duck.

To emulate the fox's success, people developed dogs that not only resembled reynard in appearance but also in action. Like a pied piper, a tolling dog could lure many unsuspecting ducks and geese into his master's clutches and thus render itself indispensable when it came to putting meat on the table.

Nicolas Denys: Drafting a Description

When seventeenth-century explorer and colonizer Nicolas Denys (1598 - 1685), in his book *Description*

and Natural History of the Coasts of North America,
wrote of the use of tolling dogs in Acadia, as the
Maritime Provinces and parts of the State of Maine
were then called, he appeared merely to be describing
an already well-known hunting practice—tolling.
Fortunately, he didn't stop there.

These same dogs, he explained, were sent to retrieve
the dead and wounded birds. With this simple
statement, Denys forever distinguished the tolling
dogs of Nova Scotia from every other canine in the
world. There is no previous record of dogs that served
this joint purpose.

Tolling, alone, had been well documented. Records
from ancient Japan already described small, amber
dogs trained to sit motionless on the shore and attract
waterfowl into the harvesting range of trained falcons.
By the fifteenth century little red and white dogs were
luring ducks into nets along the dykes and canals of
Holland. Hunters in France and Belgium had adopted
the practice. Later, great man-made trenches leading
out of lakes and ponds in England were covered with
mesh to trap ducks and geese lured up their lengths by
prancing little dogs called "pipers."

By the time of Denys' arrival in Acadia (circa 1630s)
native North Americans, too, had developed a form of
tolling. Having observed the successful hunting tactics
of red foxes, they had devised their own method of
luring ducks and geese. They would place a fox pelt on
a string between two trees in sight of waterfowl rafting
far out on the water. Then they would jiggle the pelt
across the line until the birds, attracted by it, came within
range to capture in nets or shoot with bow and arrow.

Perhaps Denys, observing the success of this strategy,
was reminded of tolling dogs he had seen at home in

*Ron MacMillan with Harbourlights Scotia Ceilidh at the
beginning of a duck hunt. (Photo Gail MacMillan)*

France. Perhaps on his next voyage to Acadia he was
inspired to bring a couple or more with him. Certainly
the dogs' compact size made them ideal for transporting
in the limited space of a seventeenth-century sailing ship.

About this same time, firearms were becoming more
popular. These innovations allowed waterfowl to be
killed at greater distances from land. Therefore, it was
advantageous to train the dogs that had attracted the
birds to retrieve them as well. Modern inventions were
leading to major changes in the scope of the tolling dog's
skills. Denys would have been well aware of these changes.

Inspired by his adventures during those evolutionary
years, Denys, when he was nearing eighty years of age,
wrote a detailed account of his days in Acadia. Published in Paris in the 1680s, the book has, for its lack of
literary merit, become a perpetual reference for
historians over the centuries.

One of these academics was Professor William F.
Ganong, Ph.D. who translated Denys' work for the

Champlain Society in 1908. In an introduction to the English version, while commenting on Denys' "defective literary instinct" and "badness of proportioning" Professor Ganong was nevertheless quick to recognize its strengths: "His [Denys'] work is . . . valuable as a reflection of the beliefs and statements current about animals at that time," he wrote.

This history was not illustrated with any sketch of Denys himself. In fact, no painting or drawing of Nicolas Denys is known to exist. The only clue to his appearance rests in his nickname, "Great Beard." Perhaps the best image that can be drawn is that of a brave, forthright man gazing out over the forests, lakes, streams, and coasts of his beloved Acadia, a little foxlike dog sitting alert and ready at his feet. Perhaps it was at such a moment that he conceived the words he later wrote: "I believe I have not altogether lost my time."

Today's fanciers of Nova Scotia Duck Tolling Retrievers would agree.

The Mystery Years

The eighteenth century was a time of turmoil for Acadia. Possession of the area passed several times between the French and English, as broken treaties and the resulting wars tossed the region into one conflict after another.

During these tumultuous years following Denys' demise, nothing more appears to have been written about the unique little tolling retrievers of Acadia. Reasons are not difficult to find. Many of the settlers who would have been raising and using the dogs were illiterate. Those few who could read and write would have been too busy eking out a subsistence to write dog stories.

Add to this the Deportation of 1755, when thousands of Acadian families were gathered up and shipped out by the British for refusing to take the Oath of Allegiance to the Crown. Some, however, escaped the Deportation and fled into the forests and marshes. In all probability, they took with them the little red dogs that could lure waterfowl, retrieve the kill, and thus, help save their masters from starvation.

It is reasonable to suppose that only those who fled into hiding in the forests and marshes would have been able to take dogs with them. Often herded like cattle aboard waiting ships with little more than the clothes on their backs, the deported Acadians would not have had the option of taking their canines along. As a result most tolling retrievers probably remained close to their south-western Nova Scotia homes with the remaining fugitive Acadian families.

The British, however, were not about to allow the lands cleared of Acadians to lay fallow for long. Anxious to re-populate south-western Nova Scotia with people they believed would be loyal to the Crown, they offered free land grants to settlers from Massachusetts. In 1761 settlers from New England began to move into the region.

A theory arose that it was these newcomers who introduced tolling dogs to Nova Scotia. Certainly there were tolling dogs recorded as having been in the Chesapeake Bay area of New England in the early nineteenth century. No evidence can be found, however, of these dogs being used as retrievers as there is in Denys' writings. In most areas of New England where tolling dogs were used, Chesapeake Bay Retrievers brought in the kill.

The question then arises as to why the tolling retriever dogs would reappear specifically in the Yarmouth region. Probably it was because there, their unique talents could be most readily used. W. Avery Nickerson, for many years one of the acknowledged masters of the art of tolling, described the lakes and marshes of Yarmouth County as "the black duck capital of the world. Most of the area's islands in winter have bare mud flats with plentiful eel grass seed. Above the eel grass, rockweed floats with the coming of the tide. This produces a fine environment for black ducks."

Add to this the fact that Yarmouth County is approximately one-third lakes which provide fresh water—the other element vital to waterfowl populations—and the stage is set for outstanding performances by Nova Scotia's tolling retrievers. After feasting all night on eel grass along the coast, the birds return at dawn to the freshwater lakes to quench their thirst and clean salt and dirt from their feathers. Here the tolling retriever dog and his master wait.

In an article titled "A Legend in His Own Pond" in the November 1979 issue of *Outdoor Atlantic* magazine, Bill Sutherland expressed the opinion that the topography of the region had been another reason for the tolling retriever's importance and development in this particular section of Nova Scotia.

"This portion of Nova Scotia was settled by Acadians," he explained. "Its topography is vastly different from many of the other Acadian settlements . . . the rolling farmlands of Chignecto and the dyked meadows of Grand Pré. These south-western Nova Scotia settlements were in a harsh land; rocky, heavily wooded, and exposed to the ever changing moods of the Atlantic. The Acadians' mainstay of survival was hunting and fishing.

"The Little River Dog was thus developed out of the necessity for survival. The objective was to develop an excellent retriever that could withstand the strong tides and cold, rough waters of the area and also bring the quarry within easy range of the musket where maximum kill could be made with a minimum of powder.

"The black duck, in particular, frequented the area in vast numbers in the fall and winter and was a very important part of the local diet. The Canadian Wildlife Surveys of 1947–50 found flocks of wintering black ducks in this area numbering twenty thousand birds. One can only guess at the size of the wintering flocks two hundred years ago but there is no doubt they would be several times larger than that figure."

In the heart of this "ducking" mecca lies the small village of Little River Harbour. Laura Bradley, archivist at the Yarmouth County Museum and Historical Research Library, describes the area:

"In the 1800s the whole area was known as Little River. Fishing was a major source of income for residents and almost everyone was Acadian. Later, well into the 1900s, four distinct little communities evolved: Melbourne, Little River, Little River Harbour, and Comeau's Hill, each small gatherings of homes. You can pass through one into the other almost without knowing it if you don't watch the road signs. Little River Harbour is the area surrounding the wharf."

Although early residents of this area might not have believed it, fame was in the offing for this modest community. In the twentieth century, Little River Harbour would become recognized as the ancestral home of the province's official dog, the Nova Scotia Duck Tolling Retriever.

— 2 —

Eddie Kenney
Un homme avec joie de vivre

The Kenney family (sometimes spelled Kinney) settled in the Comeau's Hill Little River Harbour area of Yarmouth County, Nova Scotia. With them lived a unique type of small dog. These singular little creatures would flourish under the Kenney's guardianship for over 150 years and, remarkably, become largely recognized as the progenitors of most of today's Nova Scotia Duck Tolling Retrievers.

Eddie Kenney (1874–1953), the last of the immediate Kenney family to have bred the dogs, told both his grandson Frank Nickerson and W. Avery Nickerson, another long-time tolling retriever guardian, that his father and grandfather had raised the dogs. Where the little canines had come from prior to those days in the late eighteenth century Eddie apparently never explained. No other family, however, has such a lengthy history of raising tolling retrievers and distributing them to other breeders in Nova Scotia.

Over the years, many first-time fanciers and promoters turned to Eddie Kenney for good hunting dogs and fine breeding stock. Sheriff H. A. P. Smith certainly did. Eddie himself verified this in a letter written to Col. Cyril Colwell of Halifax in June 1944. Later Colonel Colwell himself—the man who, in 1945, succeeded in having Nova Scotia's tolling retrievers recognized as a distinct breed—purchased stock from Eddie.

According to the Wedgeport Family Book, Eddie Kenney was born on February 10, 1875, (his gravestone is engraved 1874, however) and died on December 15, 1953. Although historical records are sketchy, it appears Eddie's family had been Huguenots who left France to seek refuge in Ireland. Later they immigrated to North America. In 1781 Eddie's grandfather moved from New England to Chebogue, Yarmouth County, N.S. The Kenney family settled on the most remote bit of land

Eddie Kenney with his son-in-law Alfred Trask circa late 1930s at Little River Harbour. A Little River Duck Dog is in the background. (Courtesy Audrey [Trask] Goudey)

stretching out into the sea known as Comeau's Hill.

Eddie married Hilda Stoddard on February 20, 1905, but their happiness was short-lived. After having two children, George and Ethel, Hilda died in childbirth at the age of twenty. On January 16, 1910, Eddie married Gertrude Stoddard, Hilda's sister. She and Eddie had four children, Isabel, Claretta (Etta), Lavina (Vena), and Nicky. Gertrude died on February 16, 1923, at age thirty-six giving birth to Nicky. Since they were so young at the time of their mother's death, the children were separated to live with various relatives.

"He was a wirey little man, no more than five feet five inches tall and very thin," Etta's daughter, Audrey, recalls her grandfather. "In summer he would have his hair cut so short his head appeared to have been shaved. He loved to sing and dance and tell stories and smoke his pipe. He knew lots of Steven Foster songs and could recite many of the poems of Robert Frost. He would gesture and dance and really make his recitals lots of fun. He often showed us his gold watch and told the story of how he had gotten it for saving men from a shipwreck.

"When we were youngsters staying at our summer place in Comeau's Hill, we never got to sleep in. He was always looking for us at 6:00 A.M., asking why we weren't up. I can remember him rowing us grand-children out to the Tusket Islands to fish mackerel or pick cranberries. He was in his sixties at the time and it was a good distance but he did it, singing all the way. He always had a twinkle in his eye."

For a man who seemed filled with *joie de vivre*, Eddie Kenney had, however, known his share of pain and tragedy. In addition to losing his wives, Eddie himself had once come near an early death. When he had been

a mailman delivering mail between Comeau's Hill and Wedgeport, his car (one of the few in the area at the time) had suddenly burst into flames. Eddie had been badly burned.

He had managed to drag himself to safety but since he was in a wooded area, he had to wait some time for help to arrive. As a result, he was permanently disfigured, especially his hands.

"I'm not sure what formal education he had," Audrey says. "But people were always asking his advice. He liked to read and loved politics. He was also very knowledgeable about birds and waterfowl and was an excellent marksman. I imagine that was why he was such a popular guide."

Eddie was blessed with amazingly keen eyesight, Audrey remembers, an asset in one of his favourite hobbies, bird watching. Through this interest he became involved with author Robie Tufts who was compiling his comprehensive book *Birds of Nova Scotia*. Eddie supplied specimens and information for the author about the common egret, crowned night heron, mallard, bald eagle, and sooty tern. His contributions are acknowledged in the book copyright 1962.

Audrey remembers his deep love for his dogs and that he almost always seemed to have a litter of pups around. He also had a penchant for the name Molly. Each time his current "Molly" passed away, he promptly named a pup from the next litter the same. All of the dogs shared his life and, at times, even his bed. They never became mere pets, however. As a hunting guide, Eddie had plenty of opportunities to keep their working instincts keen.

"My sister Carol and I were allowed to play with the puppies but only until they were two months old. That

Left: Sadie's first litter, born August 12, 1997. (Courtesy Andy Wallace)

Below left: One of David Wood's pups, Jake. (Courtesy David Wood)

Below right: Toller puppy "Dog Gilmore" owned by David and Valerie Lozer. (Photo Ron MacMillan)

Taffy is another of David Wood's dogs. (Courtesy David Wood)

was when our grandfather started training them for work," Audrey says.

In his later years, Eddie Kenney lived in the caretaker's cottage on the former Judge McDermot estate that had been purchased by Eddie's son-in-law, Alfred Trask. (Alfred had married Eddie's daughter Etta.) Eddie kept a skiff in the cove below the property and often rowed out to fish.

A guide and fisherman of modest means, Eddie Kenney nevertheless did his best to care for his dogs. In a letter to Col. Cyril Colwell dated March 18, 1953, Eddie told of having just lived through a hard winter with "lots of snow."

"I lost one of the little bitches with distemper," he wrote. "I had the vet but he could do nothing for her. I have only one young honey left which is very smart. Also Molly."

"About the father of these dogs," Eddie's letter continued, "I own the father, a dog that comes from one of Dr. Burton's bitches. Walter Deviller sold this dog to a Duncken in Yarmouth. He went to Ontario and I bought the dog from him. I have had him for over two years. I have a Fitzgerald who looks after him for me."

Eddie's letter raises two important questions. First, was this dog "that comes from one of Dr. Burton's bitches" a descendant of one of Senator Paul Hatfield's dogs? Senator Hatfield had been the first person to set up a tolling retriever breeding program with the goal of having the dogs recognized as an official breed by the Canadian Kennel Club. Second, was this Dr. Burton the same Dr. G. V. (Victor) Burton who had married Doris Hatfield, Senator Hatfield's daughter, and, if so, had he continued breeding his father-in-law's strain of tolling retrievers?

If he had, then the Hatfield strain had merged with the Kenney strain and probably found its way into the kennel of Col. Cyril Colwell whose dogs were the first officially recognized as the breed Nova Scotia Duck Tolling Retriever.

However, in a December 1997 conversation with Audrey Goudey, Nora Burton (wife of Dr. George Burton, Dr. Victor Burton's son,) didn't recall her father-in-law ever breeding tolling retrievers. He had Setters she recalled; she and her husband had had Little River Duck Dogs.

Their first dog, in fact, had been purchased about 1952 in Comeau's Hill from a man who Nora Burton believes was Eddie Kenney. Given the fact that this dog was named Molly, there can be little doubt of its origins.

Dr. Burton and a friend brought Molly from Comeau's Hill to its new home. When they reached their destination, they put her in a pen with some of Dr. Victor Burton's Setters.

The next morning when the caretaker opened the pen to feed the dogs, Molly escaped. Dr. Burton and the caretaker couldn't find her and became very upset.

Eventually, they located her back in Comeau's Hill. Molly had travelled twenty-two miles to get back to her former home.

She was returned to Dr. Burton's care. According to Nora Burton, Molly proved to be a good dog and had many litters for their kennel.

The second point for speculation raised in Eddie's letter is his reference to the "Fitzgerald" who was looking after Eddie's stud dog. Could this have been William "Dossie" Fitzgerald who is believed to have been the first Yarmouth breeder to ship tolling retrievers

The friendly greeting from one of Molly's descendants at Comeau's Hill, next to Eddie's old home. (Courtesy Audrey [Trask] Goudey)

to Europe? If Dossie and Eddie shared breeding stock, perhaps the ripples begun in Eddie Kenney's small kennel in Comeau's Hill Little River Harbour spread across the Atlantic and into tolling retriever stock there.

Unfortunately, written records do not exist to substantiate these possibilities.

"I suppose that the bitches will trail this spring," Eddie concluded his letter. "So I will not be expecting any pups until late in summer."

This may well have been the last litter bred by Eddie Kenney. On December 15, 1953, he passed away at his daughter Etta's home with Molly by his side.

After Eddie's death, Molly was taken to Comeau's Hill to live with one of her master's friends. The name of that friend, however, has been forgotten, Molly's fate unknown.

In researching her grandfather's life for this book, Audrey Goudey visited his old homestead on October 1, 1997. She recounts the following amazing experience.

"We went down to Little River Harbour and Comeau's Hill to visit my grandfather's grave and his old homestead," she says. "It brought back lots of nice memories, yet was somehow quite eerie.

"When we got out of the car by my grandfather's house, a Little River Duck Dog came over to greet us and lick our hands. It looked just like my grandfather's Molly.

"I'm sure it belonged to the new owners . . . but there was no one around."

Today, descendants of Eddie's Little River Duck Dogs no doubt still live in Yarmouth County. It is hoped that these unique little canines will live happily ever after in south-western Nova Scotia as well as worldwide. It is what Eddie Kenney, *un homme avec joie de vivre*, would have wanted most.

Eddie Kenney's granddaughters, Audrey and Carol Trask, with Molly's litter of Little River Duck Dogs at Comeau's Hill, 1946. (Courtesy Audrey [Trask] Goudey)

3

Nineteenth-Century Legends
of Breed Origins

During the years when Eddie Kenney's family was unobtrusively nurturing Nova Scotia's tolling retrievers in Yarmouth County, N.S., several interesting yarns developed which attempted to otherwise explain the origins of the little red dogs. For several years the Canadian Kennel Club offered the following account as a possible explanation.

In the early 1860s, James Allen of Yarmouth County purchased a Flat-coated Retriever bitch from a ship's captain who was visiting the busy south-western Nova Scotia port. Mr. Allen bred her to a Labrador. The result was a litter of excellent duck tolling retrievers.

Later, in an effort to get smaller, redder, more foxlike progeny, Allen mated several bitches of that litter to a Cocker Spaniel from the United States. The resulting pups were mainly reddish-brown and became widely used for hunting in Yarmouth County. Allen is believed to have then drawn Irish Setter bloodlines into the mix to produce the final result, the Nova Scotia Duck Tolling Retriever we know today.

A letter from the files of the late Col. Cyril Colwell of Halifax supports this theory. Dated April 12, 1944, it was written by G. H. (Harry) Allen of South Ohio, Yarmouth County. An excerpt follows:

"I remember that about sixty years ago an old uncle of mine, James G. Allen of Yarmouth and his hunting companion Andrew McGray of Little River, Yarmouth County, used this type of dog [tolling retriever] for tolling ducks, and I have always been under the impression that they originated the so-called 'breed.'

"I have heard that they obtained the first of these dogs from the product of a cross between a Labrador retriever, or some similar dog, and some sort of spaniel.

"The descendants of these original animals, have, so far as I know, run out long ago. But many others have bred dogs for tolling ducks, and these vary as to size,

The Acadian Village near Caraquet, N.B., resembles the probable early home of the Toller. (Photo Ron MacMillan)

colour, and general appearance, though most of them serve the purpose for which they are intended more or less satisfactorily.

"Actually, now-a-days, any duck hunter who owns a dog of almost any size, coloured any shade from red to light fawn, bushy or rat-tailed, which can be taught to retrieve a stick thrown from a duck blind and then retrieve a dead bird after the shooting is over, will claim he has the original and only strain of Little River Duck Dog.

"Within the last few years, R. P. Hemeon, Town Clerk of Yarmouth, has been raising what he calls Little River Dogs."

In researching this book, however, no evidence could be found of a James Allen who raised tolling retrievers.

Yet another story credits Andrew McGray with single-handedly introducing tolling retrievers to the non-native population of Nova Scotia. In 1862 while hunting waterfowl, McGray came upon a Mi'kmaq hiding in the grass and rushes along the shore. The Indian was tossing sticks across the beach for his little foxlike dog to retrieve. Far out on the water, a large raft of black ducks floated serenely on the calm surface.

Suddenly one of the birds spotted the dog. Within seconds the entire flock was paddling swiftly shoreward. Shortly they were within range of the Indian's single barrel shotgun.

McGray, impressed by this display, immediately set about obtaining that remarkable dog. He succeeded in making a trade with the Indian, who told McGray the dog was a cross between a red fox and a mongrel bitch.

This story, however, has a couple of gaping holes. Ask most geneticists and veterinarians about the likelihood

On the Little River Marsh on the Yarmouth side of Little River. (Courtesy Audrey [Trask] Goudey)

of progeny from such a mating and they will immediately assure you it is impossible since the fox comes from the feline family and the dog from the canine.

Another question that arises from this tale is like the riddle of the chicken and the egg. Was it the native people who first developed the tolling dog—legend has it they used a fox pelt draped over a line strung between two trees—or had the native people two hundred years earlier obtained them from French and Acadian settlers like Nicolas Denys?

Certainly the Acadians had managed to establish beneficial relationships with the native people of that period. Perhaps in return for information on birchbark canoes, snowshoes, and maple syrup the French and Acadians had offered their knowledge of the tolling retriever.

It is known that one of Nicolas Denys' contemporaries, Phillippe (Jean-Jacques) Enaud who settled near Bathurst, N.B., in the mid-1600s married the daughter of an important Mi'kmaq leader. Since the dogs, as described by Denys during the period, were probably part of Enaud's household, they might easily have found their way into the possession of local First Nations people.

Ambiguity warms both of these possibilities to intriguing hues. For vivid colour and outright drama, however, no other tale can equal this final explanation of tolling retriever origins. The story begins with a seafaring adventure.

Sometime during the 1800s a ship carrying a Flat-coated Retriever was wrecked during February or March off Pinkney's Point, Yarmouth County. The dog managed to swim to safety on a nearby island which was known to be overrun with red foxes.

The following autumn, Yarmouth fishermen passing near the island noticed some unusual puppies on the shore. Working in pairs (one pup twitched its bushy tail while the second lay ready to pounce when birds came within reach), the little dogs were having phenomenal success in luring and catching ducks.

Impressed, the fishermen made for shore and captured these remarkable fox-retriever puppies. They took them back to the Little River Harbour-Comeau's Hill area of Yarmouth County to become the ancestors of all Nova Scotia Duck Tolling Retrievers.

These pups were supposedly the result of a mating between that ship-wrecked Flat-coated Retriever and male foxes on the island. Since it was a widely held belief in those days that male foxes would breed with bitch dogs during the months of February and March the tale seemed plausible at the time.

All these stories considered, the oral accounts of how Eddie Kenney and his forebears established and maintained tolling retrievers in Yarmouth County are definitely the most reasonable. These alternative nineteenth-century theories are simply legends which, for more than three hundred years, have added colour and mystery to the Nova Scotia Duck Tolling Retriever story.

4

H.A.P. (Harry) Smith
Premiere Publicist

The next significant figure in the history of Nova Scotia's tolling retrievers was the antithesis of Eddie Kenney in many ways. Whereas Eddie Kenney was a modest hunting guide and fisherman with no larger ambitions than to raise fine tolling retrievers for friends and neighbours as well as himself, Sheriff H. A. P. (Harry) Smith was a flamboyant sportsman, determined to promote the dogs and establish a breeding program capable of handling the many orders for puppies he felt such publicity would generate.

Described as one of the more colourful characters Nova Scotia has ever produced, Harry Smith was at various times High Sheriff of Digby County, president of the Nova Scotia Guides Association, a respected ornithologist, an accomplished salmon fisherman, and an enthusiastic cricket player. Most important, however, from an historical perspective, he was a prolific writer for a number of the leading outdoor magazines of his day.

Henry Albert Patterson Smith was born on April 24, 1864, in Digby, N.S., the son of Dr. Peleg Wiswell Smith (1837–1880) and his wife Sarah Eliza (née Viets). Harry Smith's first wife whom he married on June 20, 1892, was Lizzie Hughes, the youngest daughter of Capt. James Hughes. He and Lizzie had two children, Clifford and Violet. Later he and Lizzie divorced.

According to his step-granddaugher Helen Matheson of Digby, Sheriff Smith was a man who not only enjoyed the sporting life but good drink and good food as well. His appreciation for fine cooking led him to meet his his second wife, Helen's grandmother.

Mary Ellen May (née Brush, having previously been married to William May) was a middle-aged widow with a grown family when she met the flamboyant Harry Smith. She was working as a cook in a sporting

The colourful, flamboyant Sheriff H. A. P. (Harry) Smith of Digby, August 1913. (Courtesy Helen Matheson)

camp where he was staying during a hunting trip.

One evening after Sheriff Smith had finished an especially satisfying supper, he asked to meet the cook. Shortly afterwards, he and Mary Ellen were married and moved into living quarters in the Digby jail.

As a divorced man and an Anglican, Sheriff Smith found his way to happiness with Mary Ellen a difficult trek. His mother, Sarah Eliza Viets, had been a member of the family of the Reverend Viets, an early pastor for Trinity Anglican Church in Digby; thus, ties to the diocese were deep. Succeed he did, however, and in the process inherited seven stepchildren.

Life with Sheriff Smith wasn't always easy for Mary Ellen. In addition to providing meals for the jail's inmates, she often found herself forced to return to her job as cook to help finance her husband's lifestyle. In all of his sporting interests he appears to have always been nattily attired.

Hunting, as photos reveal, was no exception, and out of this interest grew his involvement with Nova Scotia's tolling retrievers that were, by his time, known locally as Little River Duck Dogs. He became enthralled with the little red canines and wrote a number of articles describing them at work. One such piece appeared in the April 1918 issue of *Forest and Stream* (now *Field & Stream*).

"Although I thought I knew all there was to learn concerning the ability of the tolling dogs in assisting the gun to obtain a bag of ducks, purely by accident, I discovered not only that Canada geese would toll, but also that ducks will walk as well as swim to the dog.

Late last winter I was waiting in a blind for wild geese. As the flood tide came nearer over the immense mud flats, sixty Canada geese could be seen feeding along its edge but, with the perverseness of geese, they swam by, disappearing behind the point to the left of my cove.

"A big bunch of black ducks were noisily feeding out in front, and when the flood was reached in at about seventy-five yards from my blind, they, too, decided the danger zone was reached. After waiting until the salt tide had come to within about forty-five yards of my blind, I decided to toll them in.

"I ran my tolling dog out on the marsh behind me and he played for some minutes before the birds noticed him. At last two or three old ducks woke up and stretched their necks, announcing to others with loud quacks that something unusual was in sight on shore. In a second every duck was interested, and soon the tip end of the flock 'broke off' and swam for shore. Reaching the sand, three birds stepped on shore.

"Just at this moment I happened to glance up the bay and, to my surprise, noticed four wild geese about five hundred yards away swimming toward me as fast as their pads would propel them. It flashed through my mind that they had seen the ducks coming on shore and thought it was safe for them also. Motioning for the dog to drop beside me in the blind, I waited for their approach. However, as soon as the dog was out of their sight they began to swim away. Suddenly it dawned upon me that it was the dog they wanted.

"Picking up the 'tolling stick' I tossed it out across the sand to the marsh. Like a flash the dog was after it. I glanced through the peek-hole in the blind con-firmed my guess. Here came the four 'honkers' as straight and as fast as they could swim for the dog, and now, with the fine inconsistency of human nature, I

Sheriff Smith on a hunting expedition. (Courtesy Helen Matheson)

wished those black ducks were miles away! Here they were, right between me and the geese.

"In a few seconds every duck was on shore, standing with extended necks looking at the dog. In all my former experience in tolling ducks, I had never seen birds step out of the water upon the shore. These ducks not only stepped out, but began to waddle up toward me like a battalion of recruits on parade.

"So curious became some of the birds that they waddled up within fifteen feet of the blind, a few of them even walking around trying to peck into it, to see where the dog had disappeared. Every second I feared this inquisitive advance guard would discover me and take alarm.

"What a racket they kicked up! Whenever the dog would run in out of sight, every duck would quack in unison.

"Along came the geese and, reaching the shore, two of them stepped out. They were in line and not more than thirty-five yards away. The other two were just at the edge of the tide, watching for the dog. Rising up to shoot over the blind, I of course, scared the ducks, the whole flock jumping together in a solid bunch.

"So thickly were they packed together I could not see through them to get a shot at the geese. Hesitating, while they spread out, I at last saw two big birds flying across my right front. The first one fell with three No. 2 shots in his neck. My next shot accounted for his mate.

"The dog retrieved both of them and, running up to me, waited for his caress, which is always due him after a successful toll.

"Here I had learned two lessons in a few minutes, namely geese will toll and ducks will leave the water and walk up on shore to the dog."

In 1983 Wayne Adair, a writer for *Ontario Out-of-Doors* magazine, reported that he had seen thirteen of Sheriff Smith's original unedited manuscripts. At that time they were in the possession of Sheriff Smith's ninety-year-old son Clifford who was living in Aurelia, Ontario.

Sheriff Smith was also determined to promote these Nova Scotia tolling retrievers in deed as well as in print. In 1917 he established a tolling retriever kennel at the head of St. Mary's Bay and settled back to await orders for his pups. He believed these would come from far afield as a result of his writing.

Perhaps the best remaining description of Sheriff Smith's venture into dog breeding is embodied in a letter dated March 18, 1944, from F. A. (Fred) Graham of Digby to Col. Cyril Colwell of Halifax. Colonel Colwell had probably learned that Graham was a friend of one of Sheriff Smith's stepsons (Helen Matheson's father) and, as a result, had written to him requesting information on Sheriff Smith and his dogs.

According to Graham's letter, Sheriff Smith had hunted all the way from the head of St. Mary's Bay to Annapolis Royal as well as around the lakes adjacent to Digby. When he decided to establish a tolling retriever kennel, he chose St. Mary's Bay as its location.

With seven bitches and two stud dogs, which Mr. Graham believed Sheriff Smith had purchased from Eddie Kenney of Little River Harbour, Sheriff Smith opened his operation in 1917. The business, however, was short-lived.

"He made way of all these (dogs) at the end of three or four years," Graham wrote. "He seemed discouraged on account of a lack of orders from outside the district. He would not sell any locally."

In answer to Colonel Colwell's question, "Are there any of these tolling dogs now available [that] anyone could be sure are descended from Sheriff Smith's kennel?" Graham replied, "No. Star Patillo of Truro purchased one but I am of the opinion this dog was stolen. Leslie MacDuff also had one but I have no knowledge of him since. I had three but all have passed for one reason or another."

"I knew McDuff's dog," Colonel Colwell replied in a letter written on March 24, 1944. "He was a rangy dog, quite red, with broad white blaze and pink nose. He was shot or poisoned."

In June 1944 Colonel Colwell received a reply to a letter he had sent to Eddie Kenney of Little River Harbour on March 23, 1944. In this letter Colonel Colwell had asked if Sheriff Smith had gotten any of his dogs from Kenney.

"Yes," Eddie replied. "Sheriff Smith got all his pups from me and I am sending you some of the pictures of them. I still have the same breed and will have a litter this June. They are nearly all spoken for. I get ten dollars for them."

Helen Matheson recalls the last of the Smith strain of dog in her family as being a kindly creature called Bubbles. He eventually died of old age.

As an owner and trainer of both the old-time tolling retriever and its modern counterpart, she speaks from experience.

"The tolling retriever I had through much of my childhood was named Bigalow," she says. "He was a deep chocolate colour and had a wonderful temperament . . . very easy to train and great among children. I remember many of the tolling retriever dogs back then were either lighter or darker than today's Nova Scotia Duck Tolling Retrievers. And generally, calmer."

Unfortunately no records of Sheriff Smith's breeding programs could be found. Where these papers went after his death on April 23, 1923, at Saint John, N.B., is a mystery. Some say his canine records eventually found their way into the files of Judge Vincent Pottier and were perhaps accidentally discarded after the judge's death.

The houses where he lived in Digby remain.

In retrospect, Harry Smith can be regarded as the first publicist of Nova Scotia's tolling retrievers. He tried to tell their story well and truthfully, yet with a flare that would attract widespread interest. His stories have been described as among the best ever written on the breed. Perhaps the only time he erred was when he attempted to provide a definitive history of the breed.

In his magazine articles he is said to have supported the James Allen theory of the breed's beginnings, which was later adopted by the Canadian Kennel Club and for many years held as an acceptable explanation. Recently, however, research has revealed the dogs' history stretches much further back into Nova Scotia's past.

According to Eddie Kenney who first captioned this photo, "One of the dogs of the Sheriff Smith strain." (Courtesy the Colwell family)

This revelation does not diminish Smith's contribution toward the dogs' recognition as a distinct breed in the view of those who came after him. Other champions of Nova Scotia's tolling retrievers were swift to give Sheriff Smith credit for his ground-breaking work in canine publicity.

In a letter to F. A. (Fred) Graham of Digby on March 24, 1944, Col. Cyril Colwell, whose father had been a friend of Sheriff Smith, expressed these feelings:

"I wish H. A. P. Smith were alive today for I have a message for him which I know would greatly please him. For twenty-one years I have been trying to get this Nova Scotia Dog recognized as a distinct breed and I am happy to say that on the eighteenth of March I finalized my efforts. This information, I am sure, would have pleased Mr. Smith."

5

Senator Paul Hatfield

Beacon of a Bonafide Breed

In the 1920s Senator Paul Hatfield of Yarmouth County decided the tolling retriever dogs of his area had languished in official obscurity long enough. To remedy the situation he set about having the little red dogs recognized as a distinct breed by the Canadian Kennel Club. From the evidence available, he was the first to attempt this challenge.

Born at Chebogue, Yarmouth County, on March 13, 1873, Paul Hatfield was the son of Abraham M. Hatfield and Margaret (née Shortt) of Bangor, Maine. Abraham Hatfield was Municipal Councillor and Warden for Yarmouth for twenty years.

"Paul Hatfield came from a long line of seafaring men," *The Yarmouth Herald* once described the Senator. "His father was one of the skippers of the day when Nova Scotia was famous for her wooden ships and iron men. Captain Abraham Hatfield was one of seven brothers, all of whom guided tall ships in deep water."

Paul Hatfield began his working years fishing and farming. Then, for a time, he operated a general store in Arcadia which he had purchased from Capt. John F. MacLarren. Later he became a commission agent dealing mainly in blueberries and lobsters. He was also an insurance agent.

On August 11, 1901, he married Sadie Trefry of Arcadia. The couple had one child, Doris, who later married Dr. G. V. Burton of Yarmouth.

Paul Hatfield's political career began when he joined the Yarmouth Municipal Council and later became warden, a position he held for six years. He first entered federal politics as a Liberal candidate in the general election of 1921. He was returned to office in the elections of 1925 and 1926. In the latter year he resigned his seat to open a constituency for Col. J. L. Ralston who was to become Minister of National Defence in MacKenzie King's Cabinet. On October 7, 1926, he was appointed to the Senate.

Senator Paul Hatfield set up a Toller breeding program with CKC registration in mind for the breed. (Courtesy Yarmouth County Museum and Archives)

During these years when he was deeply involved in politics, the Senator found his main relaxation in training his Little River Dogs and hunting at his lodge on one of the Yarmouth lakes. In the 1920s and early 1930s he became interested in having these unique little dogs recognized as a distinct breed by the Canadian Kennel Club (CKC). With this goal in mind, he set up a tolling retriever breeding program.

It has not been possible to locate any of the records of Senator Hatfield's kennel. Correspondence between Dr. C. B. Sims, a veterinarian from Paradise, N.S., and Col. Cyril Colwell of Halifax during the 1940s does, however, give brief insights into the Senator's work.

Dr. Sims wrote to Colonel Colwell on February 26, 1944, "I doubt if Senator Hatfield ever wrote any material on these dogs. In fact, I think he raised them only a few years. He was in hopes some day to have the breed registered. I remember some few years ago that he had pictures published in a sports magazine of his dogs, and some notes as to the characteristics of these dogs. Other than that, I have never seen any material on this breed."

In February 1944, when Colonel Colwell was trying to determine the ancestry of a tolling retriever named Rusty with a view to having the dog registered with the CKC, he again sought Dr. Sims' help. The doctor's answer once more involved Senator Hatfield: "Senator Paul Hatfield also tried to trace this breeding (Rusty) and he, too, was not successful."

Apparently the Senator had been trying to establish the required purity of generation that would meet Canadian Kennel Club standards.

On April 12, 1944, G. H. Allen of South Ohio, Yarmouth County, offered Colonel Colwell further information on the Senator's attempts to establish a purebred tolling retriever kennel.

"Senator Hatfield tried his hand at breeding them, but the chap who looked after the dogs made a mess of the whole business and the Senator gave up in disgust. I don't know that the Senator ever wrote any articles on the subject."

Thus apparently ended the first serious attempt to have Nova Scotia's tolling retrievers officially recognized as a breed. Senator Hatfield died on January 28, 1935, at his home on Collins Street in Yarmouth.

"Senator Hatfield, remarkably sturdy for his years, had been in apparent good health until Christmas," the *Montreal Gazette* reported on January 29 of that year. "Seized with influenza then, he was confined to his home. His condition, though, did not become serious until less than two weeks ago when complications arose from a blood disease, malignant neutropenia."

The *Gazette* described the Senator as an active member of the Methodist Church first and, after church union, of the United Church. From time to time, he held offices in the congregation; for many years he was Sunday School Superintendent at the Arcadia United Church.

A dedicated sportsman, Senator Hatfield had been an enthusiastic horseman in his youth. Later he maintained a keen interest in the Yarmouth Duck and Game Association.

Speaking in the Senate on February 5, 1935, Honourable Raoul Dandurand in a tribute to the late Senator Hatfield described him in glowing terms.

"A modest man in expression of his views, preferring to listen attentively before making his decision.

"In committees, he followed closely all discussions and then gave us the benefit of a conscientious and independent judgment, for he had a well-balanced mind.

"He was a man of few words, and if it be true that we shall be held responsible for idle words that fall from our lips, I know many of his colleagues will be held accountable where he will be free from condemnation."

"Yarmouth will miss the happy smile, the cheerful voice, and the kind and friendly greetings of Paul Hatfield," wrote Henry A. Waterman, President of the Yarmouth County Liberal Association. "Senator Hatifield worked hard for what he thought was right for his constituency. He was of great value to his party. He was capable in his work and loyal to his organization. But he will be remembered most, by those who have known him best, for his constant effort to keep politics clean and to be frank and fair in his every problem. Very few persons have learned to know and understand so many people in so many walks of life as Paul Hatfield. To his host of friends, it will be long before his place can be filled."

Senator Hatfield had not succeeded in his bid to have Nova Scotia's tolling retrievers recognized by the CKC, but he had awakened the possibility in the minds of others. His farsighted idea would be brought to fruition by Col. Cyril Colwell nine years after his death.

— 6 —

V.J. Pottier
and his Touring Toller

Rumours that one of Nova Scotia's tolling retrievers named Gunner appeared at the New York's World Fair in 1938 and won a prize there still persist in Yarmouth County. And the man credited with bringing about this amazing piece of tolling retriever publicity is, according to the stories, one of Nova Scotia's prominent historic figures, Justice V. J. Pottier.

Vincent J. Pottier was born on April 11, 1897, in the small Nova Scotia Acadian community of Belleville, Yarmouth County, the son of Augustine and Rose Aimee Pottier. After attending public schools in Belleville, Eel Brook, Melrose (Massachusetts) and Yarmouth, he continued his education first at Saint Anne's College and then at Dalhousie Law School. On May 1, 1920, he was admitted to the bar and entered into a partnership with R. W. E. Landry, K.C., of Yarmouth. (Pottier himself was appointed K.C. or King's Counsel) in 1932.

By 1935, with a successful law practise in both criminal and civil law to his credit, he entered national politics to become the first Nova Scotian Acadian to win a seat in the House of Commons representing Shelburne-Yarmouth-Clare. According to a biographical article in Halifax's *The Chronicle-Herald* on February 4, 1980, "the majority of votes he won during his first election has never been equalled in the history of the constituency." He held this position over the next ten years.

In spite of a busy schedule during those years Vincent Pottier remained an ardent outdoorsman, hunting and fishing the forests and streams of Yarmouth County. With his beloved tolling retriever, Gunner, he bagged numerous ducks and geese in his home territory and developed a deep admiration for the little red dogs indigenous to south-western Nova Scotia. Inspired, he joined forces with his friend Eddie Babine, a well-known local sportsman, to set up a

Vincent Pottier and his new car, circa 1920s or 1930s. (courtesy Joan Semple)

breeding kennel in the Belleville area with Gunner as its primary stud dog.

By the early 1930s Vincent Pottier had decided these amazing dogs should be introduced to the world outside Yarmouth County. With this goal in mind, he took to the road. Promoting both south-western Nova Scotia and its tolling retrievers, he and Gunner began travelling to sportsmen's shows in New England.

Gunner is featured in photos, now in the possession of the Yarmouth County Museum, which depict him during exhibits in the 1930s in a booth set up to attract sportsmen to the area.

In 1937, when Yarmouth veterinarians had discovered Gunner had a rupture, he was taken by his concerned master for treatment in New England. There, the dog made the headlines in a Boston newspaper.

Described by the paper as a "ten-year-old mongrel collie" who had "sailed the bounding main and crossed an international border to get surgical treatment," Gunner at first puzzled his doctors by his total lack of understanding of verbal commands until they realized Gunner understood only French. Once they had discovered the problem and brushed up on the language, the staff found the little dog a model patient.

"At the leave-taking, hospital attendants said, the anguish in the dog's eyes was matched by tears in those of his owner," the paper reported. "While the animal was still under anesthesia, Pottier (a member of Parliament for his province) telephoned from Yarmouth for word of his condition."

The account ends with the optimistic forecast that "Gunner was decidedly on his way to recovery and ready for another romp with his master after a fallen duck."

This, however, had not been Gunner's first foray into print. He had already been featured in an article in the March 1932 issue *of Rod and Gun* and *Canadian Silver Fox News* by Verner Augustus Bower. The writer described Gunner as a "master toller, . . . handsomely marked, a golden reddish-brown, a trifle lighter than the ordinary dog of this strain, and with a blaze white lined face, an excellently marked white chest and white tipped on all four legs.

"Mr. Pottier, known to his sporting friends as 'Vince', assured the writer that in all his tolling throughout the year he rarely shot over a brace or two of birds at a shooting. And that there are numbers of other sportsmen equally sporting in their respect of bag limits."

Not only magazine writers sought out Vincent Pottier's expertise on the tolling retriever during those years. Generally regarded as the leading authority on Nova Scotia's Duck Tolling Retrievers during this period, Vincent Pottier, on December 10, 1936, wrote the following response to questions about the dogs posed by Evelyn Campbell, Assistant Librarian at the Provincial Museum, Nova Scotia Technical College in Halifax:

"I have before me your letter of the seventh in regard to the breed of dog known as the 'Little River Duck Toller.' I am enclosing herewith a picture of the Duck Toller, so called, that I own at the present time, showing what the average duck tolling dog looks like. The name 'Little River' comes from a place about twelve miles from Yarmouth called Little River Harbour, where it seems, the duck tolling dog was used quite extensively.

"The idea behind it all is to have a dog that looks something like a fox in colour and size, and have him play on the shore, that is, run back and forth, in sight of the ducks. This playing, for some unknown reason, amuses the ducks and they 'toll,' or, in other words, come to within a few feet of the shore where they can be shot at.

"The dog in the picture was shown at the New England Sportsmen's Show at Boston for two years. I have found that the idea was not generally known in New England and that, as a matter of fact, there were no such dogs used.

"I found on investigation, tracing the history of the dog, that similar dogs are used in England and have been used for several hundred years to toll ducks. The best book on the subject is one written by Sir Payne Galloway. I could not find any other place in the world where a dog was used for a similar purpose. In trying to trace the history back in Nova Scotia, I found that this dog is used only in western Nova Scotia. I heard of one in Sydney, I think, some time ago.

"This breed of dog was never registered and the only way to get a good duck dog is to find one coming from a stock that have been duck tolling dogs. You, of course, have to have the colour and the size, along with the instinct of playing on the shore. There are, I would say, only about a dozen good duck dogs in western Nova Scotia at the present time. There are a number of dogs that are called tolling dogs but they all have some fault. Either they will not play, will not retriever or get too excited when the ducks are near, etc., etc.

"I have written this letter in a hurried way and I will be pleased to give you any further information that you may desire. I have one or two other authorities where this dog was described. I think one of them was a book written by Dr. Phillips and the other a book written by

someone in England. I wrote to the author, asking him for certain information, but I have forgotten his name on the moment. If you would like to have these authorities, I think I could find them by going back in my files."

Justice V. J. Pottier. (Courtesy National Archives of Canada)

In September 1944 Col. Cyril Colwell, in his quest to establish the lineage of more of Nova Scotia's tolling retriever stock, wrote to Vincent Pottier. In that letter Colonel Colwell asked Mr. Pottier to sign an affidavit stating that he had purchased Gunner on May 20, 1933. Colonel Colwell's investigations had led him to believe Gunner had been purchased from William Trefry who lived on Argyle Street in Yarmouth.

"As a matter of fact," Pottier wrote in his reply, "Gunner, my old dog, was born in March 1929.… Is that the one in the affidavit that is supposed to be Gunner #1?

"Any affidavit I sign I would like to start from him. He was the best dog of any of them and I think is entitled to the credit of starting the retriever dog. I think if I did a little more digging, I could give you his father and mother and their approximate time of birth."

Whether Vincent Pottier or Colonel Colwell proceeded with the investigation into Gunner's background is not known. In September 1944 Vincent Pottier was finally forced to have Gunner put down at the age of fifteen. It was a painful blow. He and his wife

Lena had had no children; Gunner had held a special place in their hearts for close to sixteen years. It appears that Gunner's death ended Mr. Pottier's interest in tracing the dog's roots.

Vincent Pottier's own life continued with many achievements to come. In 1945 he retired from politics and in 1947 was appointed Judge of the County Court of District One in the Province; in 1950 he was named District Judge in Admiralty of the Exchequer Court of Canada and for the Admiralty District for the Province of Nova Scotia; and in 1954 he became chairman of the Royal Commission on Education Finance in the Province of Nova Scotia.

"The eighty-four page Pottier Report (on education finance) merits a place in the history of education ranking close to Sir Charles Tupper's Free Schools' Act of nearly a century before," Halifax's *The Chronicle-Herald* stated on July 27, 1974.

In 1965 Vincent Pottier was appointed Justice of the Supreme Court of Nova Scotia and of the Court for Divorce and Matrimonial Causes for the Province. Later that same year he was named Justice of the Trial Division of the Supreme Court.

Over the years, Judge Pottier also acted as mediator in a number of labour disputes, all of which were settled without strike action, and he initiated much needed changes in the treatment of the mentally ill in Nova Scotia. He had been president of the Halifax Kiwanis Club, president of the Fish and Game Association in Yarmouth, president of the Nova Scotia Historical Society, a member of the Board of School Trustees in Yarmouth, a director of the Yarmouth Hospital, and president of Alliance Français (in 1952) as well.

Judge Pottier retired on May 1, 1970. It was the fiftieth anniversary of his admission to the bar.

Vincent Pottier had married three times. His first wife whom he married in 1923 was Kathryn LeBlanc of Wedgeport. After her death he married Helena (Lena) McKinley of Yarmouth on August 10, 1928. After Lena's death, he married Sheila (Smyth) MacDonald of Halifax on October 16, 1963. There were no children from any of these marriages.

Judge Pottier died on February 4, 1980, in Halifax at the age of eighty-two. Surviving relatives were his third wife Sheila and a brother, Philomon, of Belleville. At his funeral he was remembered warmly.

"Mr. Justice Pottier was held in the highest regard by the barristers of Nova Scotia," said Bruce Nickerson, Q.C., president of the Nova Scotia Barristers Society.

Although Judge Pottier's name will doubtless find its way into many history books as a result of his numerous professional, legislative, and judicial achievements, his place in this book is secure because of his devotion to one small red dog named Gunner and his efforts to show the world what he considered one of Nova Scotia's finest products, the Little River Duck Dog (later also known as the Nova Scotia Duck Tolling Retriever).

Vincent Pottier's famous dog Gunner, March 20, 1929 - September 15, 1944. (Courtesy Yarmouth County Museum and Archives)

7

Eddie Babine

Bolstering the Breed at Home and Abroad

"From a breeder's perspective, it was probably Eddie Babine and Eddie Kenney before him who had the most influence on the early development of the tolling retriever in the Yarmouth area," says Jim Jeffery, Nova Scotia Duck Tolling Retriever historian, breeder, and sportsman.

Eddie Babine went one step further than Eddie Kenney; however, he promoted the breed abroad.

During the 1930s and 1940s, Eddie Babine, a well-known Yarmouth County contractor and sportsman, joined forces with Vincent Pottier to breed and promote Nova Scotia's tolling retriever. In a 1978 recorded interview with Jim Jeffery, Eddie said he and Vincent Pottier had bred dogs in the Belleville area for a number of years. Furthermore, he said he had accompanied Mr. Pottier to sportsmen's shows in New England in attempts to promote the dog.

Eddie described his concept of a good tolling retriever as a yellowish dog with white on the tips of tail and feet and possibly a snowy blaze on the face. He said he could train a tolling retriever with three or four days of intensive work. He had once been offered five hundred dollars for one of his trained dogs by a husband and wife from New Brunswick but had refused. First, he said it was too much money for a dog, and second, it was only a couple of days until the opening of hunting season and he wouldn't have time to train another dog.

As Remembered by his daughter Joan Semple

"Dad, Edward Laurie Babine, was borne in Belleville, Yarmouth County, on December 19, 1898, one of the six children of "Tinan" Louis Ferdinand Babine and Rosalie Aimee (née Surette). Louis was a professional building mover and was remembered in the Yarmouth area for his moving even fairly large buildings, such as

Eddie Babine and his Little River Duck Dog bringing home the rewards of their hunting. (Courtesy Joan Semple)

the Argyle Sound Baptist Church (April 1899), by his distinctive method using a capstan and a single horse.

"As a young man, Dad went to the United States as so many from the area did and later, during World War I, to France where he acted as a translator. After the war he returned to Nova Scotia, became a contractor (mainly road building) and, on October 1, 1935, married Bernadette Saulnier.

"He was almost forty at the time, an old bachelor, but from what I gather, a very eligible one with one of the few Model T cars in the area and a cottage or 'camp.' Mom was a registered nurse from Little Brook, Digby County, home on holidays and engaged to a local dentist. She met Dad, however, and the rest is history, with myself and one sister, Anne, eventually part of it.

"Mom recalls Dad, his brothers, and friends had always hunted with their four-legged companions—Little River Duck Dogs. Mom didn't accompany him; in those days, such expeditions, with a few exceptions, were regarded as all-male activities. She did, however, clean the ducks.

"The feasts that followed were special. Black ducks were such a treat! And, of course, the result of the work of a good tolling retriever.

"Our dogs were Dad's hunting companions but easily became family pets as well. We dressed them up, rode on their backs, and hung onto their tails while swimming in the lake. We never received a single nip from any of them!

"They were also extremely clever. Mom was a pretty fussy housekeeper and the dogs were never allowed in any room except the kitchen on a mat by the door or on a mat in the den. Smart dogs, they knew better than to venture further.

Joan Babine (daughter of Eddie) and Ben Trask with three of Eddie's Toller pups, circa early 1940s. (Courtesy Yarmouth County Museum and Archives)

"They weren't roamers, either. We had a large backyard, and I don't recall any of them ever leaving it.

"I remember Dad training a pup with a duck wing on a long string. He would throw the wing and then pull it towards him. The dog would sit and watch. Eventually he would be allowed to retrieve it and bring it to Dad. Dad's dogs always chased sticks, especially in the water, and dropped them at our feet.

"One trick (or convenience) Dad had taught his dogs was to urinate on command. '*Va faire Boo!*' he'd say, and the dog would immediately lift its leg. I suppose this saved time and inconvenience when the dog went with him for long distances in the car. This 'trick,' however, seemed amazing to us.

"No biography of any tolling retriever hunter would be complete without a bit of humour. Certainly my father with a reputation as a 'character' was involved in a number of comical incidents. My personal favourite was one my father used to tell of coming upon an old-time Yarmouth duck hunter sitting beside a large tub full of water and soaking his feet after a long day of 'ducking.' As he relaxed, he was enjoying a bottle of rum.

Whenever he needed a chaser, he would simply dip a cup into the tub! Dad loved to tell that story.

"Certainly, he enjoyed all aspects of the sporting life and revelled in the risks frequently involved. He took chances—daily—and Mom, a more practical person, was often unnerved by his happy-go-lucky behaviour. As a child I watched him log rolling, jumping from log to log, laughing all the while. I was terrified.

"In 1981 at age eighty-three Dad died of a heart attack while on a fishing trip. After awakening early one especially fine morning, he had roused his three younger companions so that they might enjoy the beauty of the sunrise while he prepared a big breakfast for them. (Dad was a fabulous cook and was always chef while at camp.) Soon after, as the three were portaging the canoe, Dad sat down to rest. And died.

"Bless him. He passed away exactly where he wanted to be. I will remember him fondly."

The November 1954 issue of *Saga* magazine (billed as "true adventures for men") featured an article titled, "The Dogs that Decoy Ducks." In this piece, writer Stan Smith recounted what was for him an astonishing duck hunting expedition in Yarmouth County with Eddie Babine and his tolling retriever Sparky.

Smith and Babine not only got their limit of ducks that day but also managed to shoot five geese that came in with a tolled raft of black ducks. (This incident tends to answer a question frequently posed by waterfowlers: will geese, Canadas in particular, toll? Generally no, but they will accompany black ducks into shooting range.)

Smith's story also explains Babine's venture into breeding tolling retrievers. According to the writer, Babine and his friend, Yarmouth physician Dr. Sandy Campbell, had once formed a company to set up a breeding program for tolling retrievers. They had made a motion picture film of Sparky working and had taken it, as well as the dog, to the Boston Sportsman's Show. As a result, Smith was told, orders for puppies poured in.

The magazine article suggests one of these Babine-Campbell puppies might have been the first of its kind in Russia. According to Eddie, Dr. Campbell had met some Russians while on his honeymoon to Austria and had described the amazing talents of Nova Scotia's tolling retrievers to them. When they scoffed at him, he invited them to come to Nova Scotia and see for themselves.

Shortly after Dr. Campbell's return to the Yarmouth area, he and Eddie went hunting and, by chance, met the same Russians. Eddie and Dr. Campbell invited the Russians to join them.

After witnessing the amazing performances of Eddie's dog Sparky and one owned by Dr. Campbell, the Russians offered one thousand dollars for either dog. Both men refused, but Dr. Campbell is believed to have given them a pup. That little dog could have been the first of its kind to make the long journey to Russia.

Bad news followed. After Eddie and Dr. Campbell had invested nearly one thousand dollars to set up a kennel, the Nova Scotia government decided against further promotions at the American Sportsmen's show. This decision, combined with the demands of their individual businesses, discouraged the pair of entrepreneurs. The enterprise folded.

Eddie Babine had already made himself a place in tolling retriever history. During the years he and Vincent Pottier had raised the dogs, Eddie, according to several experts, had significantly improved the breed and widened the awareness of its existence well beyond the boundaries of Yarmouth County.

8

Col. Cyril Colwell

A Man with a Mission

If there can be love at first sight, there can no doubt be fascination at first glance.
In Nova Scotia Duck Tolling Retriever history, proof exists to support this logic. The evidence follows.

One summer day in 1923, while fishing in Yarmouth County, a young man from Halifax saw his first Little River Duck Dog. He was fascinated, so much so that he would dedicate a good portion of the next forty years of his life to the propagation of the breed, documentation about it, and the eventual promotion to the status of a Canadian Kennel Club recognized breed. That man was Cyril Colwell.

Cyril Henry Colwell was born in Halifax on February 16, 1898, into a family prominent in the retail trade. Later he joined the military and achieved the rank of full colonel as a result of his service in two world wars. On October 24, 1939, he married Dorothy Wheeler of Pittsburg, Pennsylvania, whom he affectionately called "the Princess." Later the couple had two children, John and Ann.

After World War II he joined his father's firm, Colwell Brothers Ltd., in Halifax. A multi-talented man, Colonel Colwell became well known for his excellent stage performances, particularly at the Garrick Theatre. There were even rumours of offers from Hollywood. His flair for showmanship would eventually serve him well in his promotion of Nova Scotia's tolling retrievers.

Always a canine fancier, Colonel Colwell had first owned a number of exceptionally fine Great Danes. It was to the little red canines of Yarmouth County, however, that he became utterly devoted. His daughter Ann Colwell-Murdoch shared the following special memories of her father's loving care of the dogs he would eventually name Nova Scotia Duck Tolling Retrievers.

Col. Cyril Colwell of Halifax with a tolling dog. (Courtesy the Colwell family)

"Dogs were always a part of my father's life. Even when he had a major stroke and went through extensive rehabilitation, he still managed to care for his Tollers.

"Our garage in Halifax was their equipment room, their hospital, and their 'birthing' room. Many times I saw the mother, under warm lights and blankets, give birth to her litter, biting open each milky sack and letting out this little, wet, closed-eyed pup.

"There was usually one pup that was scrawny and, as is not uncommon, the mother would push it away. My father, watchful at feeding time, would take one of the healthy pups off the mother and replace it with the scrawny pup and hold it there for its feeding.

"In Queensland, at our family's summer residence, my father would make runs through the woods for the dogs. A couple of times a dog got loose. I remember one time my favourite dog, Molly, went missing for a few days. Eventually she returned and literally guided Dad back through the woods to where she had given birth. Poor Molly looked so tired and worn out that she seemed to be saying, 'Okay, I did the hard part . . . now you take over while I have a rest!'

"My father loved his dogs and wanted to show others just how wonderful they were. When the pups were old enough he would lay them in a large open basket which was lined with a gorgeous bright yellow and black tartan cashmere blanket. He would then give them their very own display window with a sign stating the breed, etc., at Colwell Brothers Ltd. on Barrington Street in Halifax. Passersby were captivated!

"Dad also purchased a white cashmere suit and stetson designed in England. A born showman, he would dress in this outfit and proudly walk his dogs. If you're familiar with the dogs' colour, you can imagine the powerful visual effect this would have."

In the process of promoting his dogs, Colonel Colwell also made 8 mm movies and showed them at work. One of the stars of his films was Rusty, a dog owned by his long-time friend William Sutherland of Lockeport, N.S. Bill Sutherland, William's son, now retired in Sable River, N.S., thinks Colonel Colwell and his father may have become acquainted during their service in World War I. Later Colonel Colwell visited Sutherland Sr. when seeking suitable breeding stock for his kennel in Halifax, and the two old friends were reunited through their common interest in tolling retrievers. Bill Sutherland recalls the results of that reunion.

Bill Sutherland Sr. hosted "the Babe" at his L'Hebert camp. (Courtesy Bill Crowell)

"I was a small boy at the time (late 1930s) when Colonel Colwell began coming to our home but I remember I was very impressed with his beautiful, well-trained dogs. Colonel Colwell and my father decided to use our male tolling retriever Rusty to breed a couple of the Colonel's bitches. One was named Fawn, I recall.

"My father had purchased Rusty from a man in Round Hill, Annapolis County. Rusty resembled a Golden Retriever-Irish Setter mix. Dogs from Rusty's bloodlines were eventually among those first registered with the Canadian Kennel Club.

One of the first registered tolling retrievers from Colonel Colwell's kennel, circa 1945. (Courtesy the Colwell family)

"Later we had one of the first registered Nova Scotia Duck Tolling Retriever pups from Colonel Colwell's Halifax kennel. We named him, appropriately I think, Colonel. This dog was a wonderful hunting companion. I recall Colonel coming ashore with two black ducks at once, one hanging out each side of his mouth. Another time he retrieved a crippled goose from wind-whipt, ice-choked water. I can still picture him tumbling end over end down a steep hill, doing battle with that goose all the way.

"Colonel was enthusiastic but at the same time cool and calculating when hunting. I remember my father even put him up on a large rock, then hid behind him as he used the dog for a blind.

"Colonel innately knew the right thing to do at the right time. He was a wonderful family pet. He never let us down."

Bill Crowell, former editor of *Bluenose Magazine*, author of several novels, and long time friend of the Sutherland family (Bill Jr. in particular) remembers the early days of tolling and tolling retrievers with the Sutherlands.

"Those were the days when Bill Jr. and myself would be going out to set up the blinds and to practise the dogs. For most of my years in the Lockeport area, I was too young to go when the gunning started."

The autumn of 1936 was especially memorable for him and Bill Jr., when baseball great Babe Ruth came to Port L'Hebert to go ducking with William Sutherland Sr.

According to the Yarmouth *Herald*, Babe Ruth had first come to the area in July 1936 for the Blue Fin Tuna Fishing Competition at Wedgeport. The story describes the home run king as constantly surrounded by admirers. It is likely he learned about the excellent ducking in the area during these encounters with local residents.

That autumn he returned quietly to the Yarmouth area and spent a week duck hunting at Haley's Lake with William Sutherland Sr. and his canine assistant, Rusty. Stories persist that it was as a result of this visit by Babe Ruth and his New York sportswriter friend Bob Edge that news of Nova Scotia's tolling retrievers spread to the United States. People such as Adolphe (Dossie) Fitzgerald of Little River Harbour are believed to have shipped Little River Duck Dog puppies south of the border in response to resultant orders.

The notoriety believed to have been given to the dogs in the late 1930s by Babe Ruth's visit can perhaps be traced to one highly influential dog. With his appearances in Colonel Colwell's 8 mm movies, association with Babe Ruth and his entourage, and siring some of the first Canadian Kennel Club registered Nova Scotia Duck Tolling Retrievers to his credit, Rusty (Suther-

land) had carved himself a niche in the history of the breed. Certainly Colonel Colwell recognized the dog for the fine specimen he was and wisely used him in his quest for Canadian Kennel Club recognition.

Colonel Colwell, however, did much more than seek out prime examples of tolling retrievers, show them off to an admiring public, and make movies highlighting their talents. Shortly after the acquisition of his first tolling retriever whom he named Man O'Peace, he became a man with a mission that consisted of two different but equally difficult goals. First, he set out to trace the origins of the tolling retriever and, second, to have the dogs recognized as a distinct breed by the Canadian Kennel Club. Both were quests that would take many years to accomplish.

Detailing possible beginnings of the tolling retriever alone was a monumental task. In the course of this research, Colonel Colwell felt impelled to investigate the legend that the tolling retrievers of Nova Scotia descended from a fox-retriever hybrid. He began with investigations close to home by sending questionnaires to several fox ranchers on Prince Edward Island.

"The opinion of one prominent fox ranch owner, a member of the Canadian Silver Fox Breeders Association, is worthy of note," he wrote after receiving replies in November 1936. "This breeder replied, 'I have never seen personally any offspring of the mating of a fox with a dog but I have heard it has happened and as foxes mate exactly like dogs and are of the same family, canine [this, according to all research available, is incorrect] there can be no doubt it can happen."

The National Research Council of Canada reply was contradictory. "The officers of the Animal Disease Research Institute of the Department of Agriculture in

Hull, Que., state that they have never known of such a mating and they think, moreover, that these would be unlikely since the fox is more nearly related to the cat family. Cats are quite frequently used to mother foxes."

Then came this surprising reply in December 1936 from the United States Department of Agriculture, Bureau of Biological Survey.

"With respect to your inquiry as to the mating of a fox with a dog, the only record that we have is that of a dog mating with a fox and producing an offspring in Germany. The male German red fox was bred to a small Pomeranian. The young were born in the Zoological Gardens near Munich."

Intrigued, Colonel Colwell was quick to follow up on this clue. On January 20, 1937, he received the following reply from H. Finck of Munich, Ger.

"In the Hellabrumn Zoo [Munich] there is a hybrid born of a European red she-fox as mother and a small Spitz [Pomeranian] as father. The animal combines, as a matter of fact, the characteristics of both its parents. It is, without doubt, a hybrid as its mother is a fox. After the animal had grown, we gave him a mate, a little prairie she-wolf [coyote] and the coyote quite singularly had young [by the hybrid] whose colour is red. The pups have proved prolific among themselves again, and of these, only one, a male, has the colour of the grandmother, the coyote."

Colonel Colwell analyzed all of these replies and came to the following conclusion.

"So many stories have been told relating to the mating of the fox with a dog and due to the fact that it was a common occurrence for wild foxes to be found in the decoys of England as well as their occasional

Colonel Colwell, in his famous white cashmere suit and Stetson, walking his Tollers. (Courtesy the Colwell family)

appearance on the shore of duck inhabited lakes in Nova Scotia that people have been led to believe this mating [took] place. No information has been found regarding the ability of the red fox to retrieve. It would appear that the [difference in the] number of days of gestation between a vixen and a bitch should have a very decided bearing against the theory of . . . the mating of the two. And so it goes that while this point in question has been proven conclusively to have been carried out in one instance, it is the opinion of the writer that there is no fox blood in our Nova Scotia Tolling Retriever dogs."

By the mid-1950s Colonel Colwell was investigating the probability of the dogs having European roots. In this research he contacted Baronesse van Hardenbroek in the Netherlands. She raised *Kooikerhondjens*, a type of dog to which Colonel Colwell believed Nova Scotia's tolling retrievers bore a resemblance both in appearance and function.

These dogs were also known as pipers since, before the introduction of gunpowder into the western world, they had been used to lure ducks up canals or pipes until they could be trapped in a net. The name *Kooikerhondjens* as it was spelled in the Netherlands, came from two Dutch words, *hondje* meaning small dog and *kooiker* meaning duck trapper.

A Dutch dog show judge whom Colonel Colwell contacted disputed the existence of *Kooikerhondjens* as a distinct breed. P. M. C. Toepoel, a respected dog show official, believed that when a *kooiker* needed a dog he simply chose a very clever small spaniel not of any particular breed.

Undeterred, Colonel Colwell continued working on his theory of Dutch roots for Nova Scotia's tolling retrievers. He began to consider the possibility that some of these dogs had found their way to North America between 1492 and 1575. "Do you suppose that when John Sebastian Cabot sailed out of St. Mayo on his second trip to New France, he carried this [type of] dog with him?" he asked Mr. Toepoel in a letter dated August 12, 1954.

At that time Colonel Colwell was probably closer to the link missing between tolling dogs of Europe and the tolling retrievers of Nova Scotia than he realized. He knew Eddie Kenney well and as correspondence verifies, had purchased breeding stock from him on

several occasions. Had he ever questioned Kenney about the dogs' origins? Certainly he did attempt to trace Sheriff Smith's dogs through the Comeau's Hill Little River Harbour breeder. Correspondence to this effect exists.

Moreover, it is possible some of the fifteen dogs originally registered with the Canadian Kennel Club in 1945 were of the bloodlines of Eddie Kenney's small kennel. As a result, some of Nova Scotia's genuine grass roots tolling retrievers may have been the ancestors of those first registered with the CKC as Nova Scotia Duck Tolling Retrievers in 1945. Definitely most of Colonel Colwell's breeding stock came from south-western Nova Scotia.

Over the years, Colonel Colwell tirelessly combed Yarmouth County searching for prime examples of tolling retrievers to add to the bloodlines of the tolling retriever kennel he had established in Halifax, and he kept detailed records. He had also taken photos of many of the dogs and carefully labelled them. Finally, in the early 1940s, he had written a breed standard and coined the breed name Nova Scotia Duck Tolling Retriever.

In 1945 Colonel Colwell's hard work was rewarded. In a letter dated March 21, K. Corley, Secretary of the Canadian Kennel Club informed him, "That in view of the evidence submitted, the breed, Tolling Retriever, be added to the list of breeds recognized by the Canadian Kennel Club and be listed under Group 1, Sporting Dogs."

Colonel Colwell died on June 6, 1965. Although he had not been an avid hunter (he once said he had only shot two ducks using tolling retrievers), he left a legacy to dog fanciers worldwide who did enjoy the sport or simply the companionship of this remarkable little

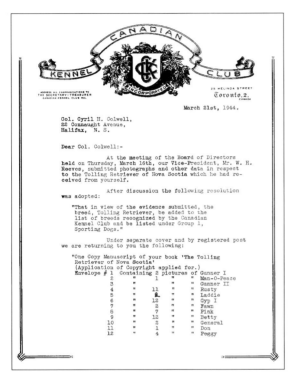

Pages one and two of the letter from the CKC marking recognition of the tolling retriever as a distinct breed to Colonel Colwell. (Courtesy the Colwell family)

dog. Colonel Colwell summed up his feelings on his many years of fascination with Nova Scotia's tolling retrievers as follows:

"What greater sportsmanship could be exemplified than to hang up our scatter guns and archery equipment, just take along a good tolling retriever, a lunch, tidbits for the dog, and an amateur motion picture camera.…Then, on a cold winter's night, when the fireside is cozily dying down and a doubting hunter calls, show him on a silver beaded screen the kind of sportsman you are. The result will be more admirers of this most amazing breed of dogs and next season we will have more ducks, dogs, and cameras and fewer guns. What a happy solution towards the preservation of two of our national resources, our dogs and our wildlife."

Bill Sutherland Jr. recalls the pleasure of making those movies. He also remembers Colonel Colwell's repeated, sincere invitations to the Sutherland family to visit his home in Halifax to view them. "He was a fine man," Bill Sutherland sums up the colonel, his tone leaving no room for doubt.

Forty years of fascination with his remarkable four-legged friends had come to a satisfying conclusion for Colonel Colwell. Both his goals had been realized. He had succeeded in having his beloved tolling retrievers recognized as a distinct breed and, in doing so, had amassed a detailed history of the dogs that is regarded as invaluable by today's fanciers of Nova Scotia Duck Tolling Retrievers.

9

The Armstrongs

Leaving a Legacy

The Nova Scotia Duck Tolling Retriever has often been referred to as Nova Scotia's best kept secret, and with good reason. For many years most grass roots tolling retriever breeders and hunters in the south-western part of the province were in no hurry to share their amazing little red dogs with the rest of the world. While never mean or tight-fisted with information or even puppies, these Yarmouth County residents felt no urgent desire to bring their dogs to national or international attention. The Armstrong family of Bellneck is a prime example.

In spite of this innate reticence on the part of their original owners, two little dogs from the Armstrong's kennel did make tolling retriever history. Purchased by Hettie Bidewell of Moose Jaw, Sask., Flip and Lady were sent west by train in the early 1950s. Mrs. Bidewell had seen a short article in the December 3, 1951, issue of *Time* magazine about the Armstrongs and their dogs and had been thoroughly intrigued. As a result she had placed an order for two puppies. These little dogs became the foundation for the tolling retriever stock at Mrs. Bidewell's famous Chin-Peek Kennel.

Late in the same decade the descendants of these two little Armstrong dogs from Bellneck became the first Nova Scotia Duck Tolling Retrievers to be registered with the Canadian Kennel Club since Colonel Colwell's famous fifteen in 1945. By the time of Mrs. Bidewell's registrations, all of the original fifteen dogs had died and no more had been registered; therefore, the process was much like starting from scratch.

Over the years, however, Mrs. Bidewell's efforts have been justified. Today many kennels breeding Nova Scotia Duck Tolling Retrievers across the United States and Canada can trace their dogs' origins back to Mrs. Bidewell's kennel and ultimately to Flip and Lady. Some Flip-Lady descendants were bred with dogs from Eldon Pace's Schubendorf Kennel in Shubenacadie,

Paul Armstrong of Bellneck and his wife Bernadette bred tollers for almost twenty years. They share fond memories of their dogs. (Courtesy Yarmouth County Museum and Archives)

N.S., and went on to excel in obedience trials. According to Toller expert Jim Jeffery, dogs from this strain "are so easy to train almost anyone could do it with a minimal effort."

The amiable personality of these little dogs is easy to understand once one becomes acquainted with the Armstrong family. Bred, born, and raised for more than fifty years close to these people, the little tolling retrievers of Bell Neck could be nothing less than friendly, gregarious, and great hunters with a rollicking sense of humour. Fred and Paul Armstrong, together with their wives Theresa and Bernadette, were affectionate caregivers to this exceptional bloodline for many years.

Paul and Bernadettte Armstrong

Paul and Bernadette Armstrong of Bellneck have loved and protected Nova Scotia's tolling retrievers for more than twenty years. The enrichment the little red canines have added to their lives is mirrored in every memory the couple, now in their eighties, relate.

Paul Armstrong, born in 1911, was the third son of John and Clara (née McBride) Armstrong, the only English family in Bellneck in the early 1900s. Paul began "ducking" when he was fourteen. By that time he owned Gyp, his first tolling retriever.

Later Paul joined his father in his blueberry business, then went on to be a carpenter and a contractor. On October 11, 1948, he married Bernadette Bourque of Eel Brook.

A young teacher with an engaging sense of humour and whose enthusiasm for ducking and tolling retrievers matched her husband's, she was well suited to be the wife of this avid hunter. Her "ducking" time

became reduced, however with the births of the couple's six children: Johnny, Tommy, Michael, Dale, Karen, and Paula.

Although the couple have not owned a tolling retriever since the early 1980s when the last one was killed by a car, their many memories of the little Yarmouth County canines glow with warmth and affection.

"As long as Paul can remember his family had a tolling retriever dog," Bernadette says. "But his interest in breeding dogs only started after we were married. Our first tolling retriever was Dusty. He was named after a country singer who was making an appearance in the Yarmouth area at the time we got the puppy. He became my all-time favourite of the dogs we had."

Paul maintains, "These dogs are special because of their temperament and natural retrieving ability. They're also good house dogs, they don't bark much and are always friendly and easy to train. Even as puppies, most of them would heel naturally."

"They're definitely natural retrievers," Bernadette agrees. "I remember small puppies picking up straws in the yard as if they were objects to be retrieved.

"Of all the dogs he's owned over the years, Paul's favourite was our last dog, Ginger, probably because he was the best behaved in the woods. Some dogs would stray and have to be called back. But Ginger just crawled into the blind right beside him.

"Paul enjoys telling the story of how Ginger, very dirty, came to him one day while he was working outside. 'Ginger, you can't come into the house this dirty. You know Mom won't allow you,' he told the little dog. Almost immediately Ginger disappeared. When he came back some time later, he was clean as a

Donald Armstrong standing in front of a blueberry truck, Bellneck.

whistle. Paul claims, that after he spoke to him, the dog ran down to the lake (we lived by the lake) and swam around until he was clean!

"As for training the dogs, Paul had no special methods. It seems these dogs were born with the knack of doing what they were supposed to. Paul would simply start very early throwing little sticks for them to retrieve. The dog would fetch it, and Paul would make sure that it would bring it back to him and not start chewing on it like puppies are prone to do.

"Paul has a kind of sixth sense when it comes to ducking. He would come home from work and say, 'I hear ducks.' He would take his gun and dog and come back later, usually with his limit of ducks."

"I remember one especially good toll," Paul elaborates. "It was a really windy day. No one but my brother Fred and I were willing to go out. On the back of an island we got nineteen ducks on a single toll."

A canny hunter herself, Bernadette has one tolling tip she believes to be of paramount importance. She stresses the ducks must *never* see the hunter. Hunter and tolling retriever must crawl into the blind even if this involves such obstacles as rocks, stumps, and puddles.

"We got our first breeding stock on Surettes Island and after that, raised tolling retrievers for almost twenty years," she says. "Not on any large scale . . . usually one litter of about four or five puppies a year."

"We don't know whether these dogs were always a part of Acadian life in Yarmouth County," she concludes. "All we know is that they certainly date way back when."

The Armstrongs never got involved in efforts to have the dogs recognized by the CKC. They were content just to breed friendly little dogs that were great hunting

Members of the Armstrong family, Bellneck, with Toller puppies. (Courtesy Paul and Bernadette Armstrong)

companions. They included Sally, Ginger, Darky, Gunner, Queenie, Dusty, and Sparky among their favourite companions. No three-name kennel labels were necessary to give these little canines status in their eyes.

Paul and Bernadette Armstrong's contribution to the fabric of Yarmouth County life has not been confined to raising a fine strain of tolling retriever. For thirteen years Bernadette was a school librarian and Paul, most of his life, a busy contractor building a number of schools and one entire section of the town which he described as "having a church at one end and a liquor store at the other."

Fred and Theresa Armstrong

Born on November 19, 1907, at Bellneck, Yarmouth County, Fred Armstrong, the eldest of the family, attended a French school and quickly picked up the language. Later he began helping his father with his blueberry business in summer and his logging enterprises in the winter.

In 1934 he married Theresa Surette on September 25. For a honeymoon, they boarded the Yarmouth boat and took a five-dollar round trip to the United States. Then they returned home to Bellneck to take care of a unique wedding gift Theresa had received.

That gift had been the result of a pact she had made a few years earlier. She and her chum Eddie Babine made a deal between them that whoever married first would have to receive a wonderful gift from the other.

Theresa went to the altar first and Eddie did indeed deliver a remarkable gift. He gave her a little tolling retriever. After that, for the next forty-five years, Fred and Theresa always owned at least one of these dogs.

For the first thirteen years of their marriage, Fred and Theresa lived in Bellneck. During that time they had three children, Donald, Jeanne, and Carol. It was while they were living in Bellneck that they were involved in breeding tolling retrievers. Later, when they moved to Yarmouth, they were only able to take one dog with them.

In Yarmouth Fred had become the first manager of the Unemployment Insurance Office in 1939. From 1946 to 1962 he operated automobile dealerships. In 1962 he was elected the Member of Parliament for his riding.

Although Theresa enjoyed the glitter and excitement of Ottawa, she was always anxious to return to Yarmouth County, which was dear to her heart.

Fred passed away on November 2, 1990. Theresa admits, sadly, that she has not had a dog for several years. She recalls, with an ache in her voice, how her last dog, a friendly little creature, was unnecessarily maced by a delivery man and how terrible it was to see the small dog rolling about in agony on the lawn. After that, she felt it was not fair to the dogs she loved so

One of Fred Armstrong's tolling retrievers, Bellneck. (Courtesy Yarmouth County Museum and Archives)

much to subject them to the dangers and stresses of town life.

Today, the Armstrong family is modest about their contribution to the breed's development. They credit Vincent Pottier and his travelling tolling retriever Gunner with arousing the international interest in the dogs that drew American attention to their Bellneck Kennel. They look for no kudos for themselves. They are content with the years of wonderful memories the little red dogs have given them and to leave an enriched legacy to fanciers of Nova Scotia Duck Tolling Retrievers everywhere.

10

Dick and Ralph Crowell

Tollers—Tools of their Trade

Dick Crowell and his youngest son Ralph were acknowledged masters of the art of tolling in Yarmouth County for well over a half century. The late W. Avery Nickerson, who has himself been called the Babe Ruth of tolling, regarded Dick Crowell as his mentor. Avery once described Dick as the best tolling man ever.

Dick's youngest son, Ralph, however, very nearly had his tolling career nipped in the bud when he went on his first hunting trip with his father. As the ducks plunged their heads under water to feed, sticking their rear ends up in the air, Ralph did the almost unforgivable. He laughed.

"If you're going to carry on like that, you won't be allowed to come again," Dick scolded his twelve-year-old son.

Although he spent his adult years in Yarmouth County, Dick Crowell had been born in Malden, Massachusetts on May 9, 1892. His parents were John Crowell and Althea Robert. Dick later moved to Argyle Head where he lived until his death in 1971.

In 1914 he married Delilah Belle Jeffery of Overton. The couple had three sons: Bernard, Ken, and Ralph, as well as four daughters, Agnes, Alice, Hazel, and Nellie.

A farmer and lobster fisherman, Dick owned his own boat which he used for fishing lobster in Yarmouth Bar. He also fished eels and developed a small business that included shipping them to Boston. This enterprise was later carried on by his son Ralph and Ralph's daughter Dianne Crowell.

Well known throughout Nova Scotia as an excellent hunter and guide, Dick became caretaker of the Argyle (hunting) Lodge in 1940. This lodge where Dick and later Ralph worked as guides and caretakers was built by an American, Ernest Brown. Brown was a businessman who had already established a chain of lodges in Quebec. He expected the best from his employees; therefore, a good tolling retriever was an essential part

Ralph Crowell and a dog identified as Gunner, but not the same one as Pottier's Gunner, on a hunting trip. (Courtesy Yarmouth County Museum and Archives)

of his guides' outfits.

"Dad once paid one hundred dollars for a tolling retriever in the mid-1960s," Dianne Crowell, Ralph Crowell's daughter recalls. "It was a tremendous amount of money for a dog in those days. I remember Dad putting the money out on the table and being totally astounded by the sheer enormity of the amount. We weren't poor but we weren't rich either so that one hundred dollars represented a large investment . . . an investment in working equipment necessary for Dad's job."

Ralph's salary was a dollar a day when he began guiding; black ducks could be sold for one dollar a pair. Ralph guided many competent hunters, but he recalls a few who could be downright dangerous with firearms.

Ralph recounts an incident in which a double triggered rifle was accidentally discharged by a client in a canoe Ralph was piloting. The bullet ripped through the stern of the canoe just above the water-line, narrowly missing the guide.

"Some [clients] didn't understand firearms," Ralph says. "That made things dangerous at times. But, then, we all took risks in those days."

Ralph owned several fine tolling retrievers over the years, Rex, Chum, and Buddy were among them. He came to be an expert both on the dogs and the art of tolling as had his father. Ralph believes not all tolling retrievers can be developed into good gun dogs and isn't sure why.

"You can't train them all," he says sagely. "Some are gun-shy for no apparent reason. You can't get a toll with a poor dog. You can usually tell when the dog is six or seven months of age if you've got a good one."

Avery Nickerson, breeder of world famous hunting tollers, shared Ralph's opinions. One of Ralph's recent Tollers was Zack, bred by Avery and Erna Nickerson at

Louise and Ernest Brown in the blind with their guide Dick Crowell and his Little River Dog, circa 1940s, Argyle. (Courtesy Yarmouth County Museum and Archives)

their Harbourlight Kennel.

Ralph stresses that a tolling retriever must be well trained. The dog must sit quietly when taken in a canoe and learn to crawl behind the hunter into the blind. "Late in the season sometimes, ducks won't come in to a Little River red dog. You may have to change to a black dog if the snow is on. Ducks are smart. They get used to seeing the red dog, get aggravated by it, and won't respond. Sometimes they won't come in anyway. If you start quacking hard, it might bring their heads up and make them notice the dog, but sometimes they just refuse to toll at all."

Sometimes, too, a dog will draw the ducks in too close for a good shot, a shot that has room to spread. Then they must be driven out a bit. The ducks should be at least twenty-five to thirty feet away. Ralph Crowell calls a good toll one that nets between ten and fifteen birds.

He offers this tip for hunters who want to be sure their tolling retriever is well out of the way when the shooting starts. Simply toss the stick, or any object you have been using as a tolling fetch, ten or fifteen feet back into the woods. By the time the "1-2-3" or "1-2-fire!" orders are over, the dog will have returned with it, the shooting will be over, and the dog is ready to begin retrieving the kill.

Like any fine craftsman, Ralph advocates respecting one's equipment and colleagues. Since his tolling retrievers fall into both categories, his concern for them is doubly sincere.

"If a dog gets too eager and jumps into the water after the ducks before you fire, *never* try to shoot over him," he says fervently. "Get the dog back in the blind, quiet him down, and toll again if you have to."

Ralph's concern for the dogs' welfare extends far beyond the hunting season. Over the years, he has taken in a number of abused or unwanted tolling retrievers.

"Dad loves the dogs," says his daughter Dianne. "He can't bear to see them mistreated. I recall one dog he brought home that had been so abused it absolutely refused to come indoors. Dad never gave up. He coaxed and soothed this frightened little dog until, at last, it would come into our garage. It was an unusual little creature in appearance with a tail more closely resembling that of a red fox than a dog."

These days the Crowell family continues the tradition of owning and protecting Nova Scotia's tolling retrievers in Yarmouth County. Both Ralph and Dianne Crowell still own dogs and hunt with them. Like most other tolling retriever people in the Yarmouth area, both feel that what really makes the little red dogs special is their friendliness. Ralph calls them a family dog, while Dianne goes one step further and links their amiable personalities to their superb tolling abilities.

"It's the desire to please their master or mistress that brings the dog back into the blind fetch after fetch when tolling," she says. "This innate dedication makes them ignore the ducks or geese until they are specifically asked to retrieve the birds."

Dick Crowell and Gunner (not to be confused with Pottier's dog of the same name). (Courtesy Yarmouth County Museum and Archives)

"I have always been more of an observer than a hunter," Dianne continues. "And now we all choose the dogs as our companions because of their wonderful personalities. My dog JesSea is now thirteen and, although stiff at times, still travels the province with me on business trips. Service station attendants where I regularly stop for gas keep treats for her. If she's not with me, they always ask about her. I believe this happens not simply because I'm a regular customer but because the bond between us is apparent and important."

Dianne is vehement in her desire to protect tolling retrievers from owners who do not understand these unique canines. JesSea is her friend and companion just as her father's and her grandfather's dogs were to them. When Ralph Crowell laid down that hundred dollars for a tolling retriever thirty years ago, he knew he would be getting his money's worth and more. He, like his father before him, knew that in buying one of these little dogs he was getting not only a workmate and companion but also a family member and a friend. In Dianne Crowell, these beliefs continue into a third generation.

11

Eldon Pace
Briefly but Better

"Eldon Pace is one of the few Nova Scotia Duck Tolling Retriever breeders of his time who seemed to understand the science associated with animal breeding," one tolling retriever expert commented. "Although his involvement was short-lived, his contribution to the breed is immeasurably large, positive, and long lasting, at least equal to Hettie Bidewell's. In fact, there are few Tollers today that don't have the Shubendorf name somewhere in their pedigree."

Ducks Unlimited has also lauded Eldon, calling him an unsung hero of wildlife conservation. No one who knows Eldon can dispute this claim. With nearly forty years as supervisor of the Nova Scotia Wildlife Park behind him and many more as a rescuer of sick, wounded, and orphaned wild animals to his credit, he definitely qualifies as a blue ribbon conservationist.

Eldon Pace, however, is an acutely modest man. Presently living in retirement in Shubenacadie, N.S., he needs no laurels to crown his many achievements. Seeing a motherless fawn survive under his care, an injured deer restored to health, or an indigenous breed of dog improved have been sufficient rewards for him.

Born in Glen Margaret, N.S., in 1925 Eldon developed an interest in all living creatures at an early age. He once said his involvement in wildlife started when he was three years old. His father had taken him to feed a flock of wild Canada Geese on St. Margaret's Bay near their home; from that day, his fascination grew. Later in his life, his chosen profession would allow him to work closely with the creatures he found enthralling.

In the 1940s he became a forest ranger assigned to the Shubenacadie Fire Station midway between Halifax and Truro, Nova Scotia. There he saw the pain and suffering often inflicted on wildlife living near a major highway. His compassion was immediate and active.

Eldon Pace, founder of the Shubendorf Kennel, made lasting contributions to the Nova Scotia Duck Tolling Retrievers. (Photo Scott Smallwood)

Soon he was caring for the sick as well as the injured animals that happened his way. Eldon lost many nights' sleep as he stayed up tending his patients. He even led recuperating deer on evening walks to exercise them before sending them back into the forest. At one point, he was involved in bottle-feeding twenty-eight fawns.

Eldon's makeshift hospital began to attract tourists and sightseers. In 1949, impressed by Eldon's dedication and the interest he and his animals had aroused, the then Nova Scotia Department of Lands and Forests decided to set up a wildlife park on the land behind the fire station. With Eldon and his wife living on its border and Eldon appointed Park Supervisor, it was an ideal arrangement.

Tending animals at the park gave Eldon an opportunity to delve into one particular area of his wildlife studies, the life and habits of brant, a variety of small, wild goose. His work with these birds, according to Ducks Unlimited, has been scholarly and led to "much information about these birds that was never known before." Certainly a book could be written on Eldon's extensive work with brant and his efforts to restore them to eastern Canada.

In 1960 Eldon's interest in animals expanded to include the Nova Scotia Duck Tolling Retriever. His first dog breeding program had begun in 1958 with German Shepherds. He had named his kennel Schubendorf in recognition of the dogs' Germanic origins, *Schuben* for Shubenacadie and *dorf* meaning town.

When he decided to include Nova Scotia Duck Tolling Retrievers in his breeding program, he purchased a single pair of dogs. The bitch that he purchased from Avery Nickerson he named Goldie; the stud dog purchased from another Yarmouth breeder he named Major. Soon he and his friend Avery Nickerson were preparing to have their dogs registered with the Canadian Kennel Club.

After Col. Cyril Colwell's registration of fifteen dogs in 1945 no more Nova Scotia Duck Tolling Retrievers from Nova Scotia had been recorded with the CKC until Eldon and Avery got together to set up breeding programs which would be recognized by the governing canine association. It was not an easy task. It required copious paperwork and many visits by CKC officials to the Nickerson Kennel in Yarmouth and the Pace Kennel in Shubenacadie to establish their stock as purebred.

By 1966 Eldon's Schubendorf Nova Scotia Duck Tolling Retrievers were well established. He and Hettie Bidewell had exchanged some dogs and these formed what has been described as the Chin-Peek-Schubendorf line. Noted for their pleasant temperaments and easy trainability, Eldon's dogs were also excellent hunters.

His knowledge of the Nova Scotia Duck Tolling Retriever is exceptional. Eldon has a keen insight into the dog's temperament, purpose, and capabilities. This knowledge is reflected in the excellent progeny that came out of his kennel.

"The Nova Scotia Duck Tolling Retriever is docile and somewhat timid until put to work," Eldon described his dogs to writer Edwin Coleman of *Rod and Gun* magazine in 1966. "Then it appears to change into a completely different animal. They are very good retrievers from both land and water and have a very soft mouth. They are non-roamers and will fight other dogs only as a last resort. They are exceptionally good with children and this does not in the least spoil them for hunting."

Eldon's goal was to produce a small, foxlike dog generally about forty pounds. He felt that the dogs were meant to resemble a red fox and that if a hunter wanted a big retriever he should purchase a Labrador, Chesapeake Bay, or Golden Retriever.

When Eldon ceased breeding Nova Scotia Duck Tolling Retrievers in the 1970s, he took his remaining dogs to Avery and Erna Nickerson's Harbourlight Kennel in Yarmouth. Thus, the Chin Peek-Schubendorf line was united with those of Harbourlight, formerly known as Green Meadows Kennel.

Presently in his seventies and retired from his position as supervisor of the Nova Scotia Wildlife Park, Eldon Pace continues to work with wild birds and devote long hours each day to their preservation and protection.

He once commented to reporters: "How many people can do the thing with their lives that they wanted to? Very few. Sometimes I feel I'm one of the luckiest people in the world."

Fortunate, too, are Nova Scotia's wildlife and provincial dog. They have benefitted greatly from their acquaintance with Eldon Pace.

W. Avery and Erna Nickerson

The Longevity of Love

Of all the people involved with the tolling retrievers of Nova Scotia, few can equal the years of dedication given to the breed by Avery and Erna Nickerson of Harbourlight Kennel in Yarmouth. Their story began during the 1930s when a teenager was given an eighteen-month-old tolling retriever pup named Chum.

Boy and dog became comrades, genuinely suited to each other through a mutual love of waterfowling. That wily pup was to inspire in the young man such admiration for the little red dogs that he would devote a generous portion of his life to their protection and refinement. The young man was W. Avery Nickerson.

So intense did Avery's love of dogs and all the paraphernalia of waterfowling become, he admitted his schooling and his obedience to his parents suffered. The little red schoolhouse he attended was located near a prime "ducking" area, and each autumn his attention to all things academic vanished with the echo of the first shotgun blast. Likewise his compliance to his father's wishes for punctuality at suppertime.

After a stint in the navy during World War II, Avery returned to Yarmouth County where he had been forced by active duty to leave his bride, Yarmouth school teacher Erna (née McCullough) Nickerson. Chum was gone by then but Erna was ready and willing to support her husband's continuing dedication to the tolling retrievers. Later the couple would have four children: Kathy, Diane, Wade, and Edwin.

"There were only a few of us looking after the dogs during those years," Avery described the Nova Scotia Duck Tolling Retrievers' lean years during the 1950s, when the only registered dogs of the breed belonged to Hettie Bidewell of Saskatchewan.

His choice of words is important. He, like Eddie Kenney, felt he was a caregiver, someone entrusted to protect and maintain a unique and remarkable

Probably Erna Nickerson holding three pups from Buffy's litter, standing in front of Avery Nickerson's house. (Courtesy Yarmouth County Museum and Archives)

creature. Avery, in fact, knew Eddie Kenney and had relatives in Comeau's Hill and Little River Harbour. When he and Erna decided to breed tolling retrievers, it was in these two small communities that they found their first breeding stock. From those early days, when, in Erna's words, they "bred a few pups from time to time" for their own hunting use, the kennel grew in size and reputation.

By the early 1960s Avery and Erna decided to look into CKC registration for their dogs. They named their kennel Green Meadows at first but later, when they moved to Overton, changed it to Harbourlight. Their first registered bitch was Autumn Cinderella, their first registered stud dog, Champ. Champ and Cindy became the foundation stock for what would become the internationally famous Harbourlight Kennel of Yarmouth County.

This success, however, was the result of many years of selective breeding by the Nickersons. Through careful planning, Avery and Erna developed dogs that were handsome, tough, and intelligent. With Avery's passion for "ducking" their hunting instincts were kept sharply honed as well.

New bloodlines later introduced into the Harbourlight strain only increased these desirable traits in the dogs. In the late 1970s when Eldon Pace disbanded his Schubendorf Nova Scotia Duck Tolling Retriever Kennel, he brought his dogs to Avery and Erna. This combined the three major bloodlines of registered Nova Scotia Duck Tolling Retrievers: Schubendorf, Chin-Peek, and Harbourlight.

Avery and Erna focused the goals of their breeding programs for these combined bloodlines on developing a small, compact, "chestie" dog with white markings on face, chest, paws, and tail. To accomplish the colouring, they mated a dog from a pure red line (exemplified by one of their finest dogs, Harbourlight Big Splash) with a dog with strong white accents.

In spite of many successful breeding strategies such as this colouration example, Avery and Erna were at the same time ever alert to what they saw as undesirable traits in their dogs. Interviewed in the late 1970s, Avery expressed a desire for his dogs to be smaller. He felt the CKC standard as laid out in 1945 had led to the breeding of larger, redder dogs in attempts to meet the official requirements of the breed. Many owners of Harbourlight dogs, however, felt that Avery and Erna's dogs were stronger retrievers as a result of their stand-ard size, more able to stand up to the rigours of "big water" retrieving than the smaller variety that were more at home in lakes and small rivers.

This large size of Harbourlight dogs definitely did

not deter buyers and breeders far afield from Yarmouth County. By the 1980s dogs from Harbourlight Kennel were achieving international fame. Breeding stock from Avery and Erna's kennel were shipped to England and Scandinavia to become the foundations of many European Nova Scotia Duck Tolling Retriever kennels.

As a result of Harbourlight's growing excellent reputation and the owners' acknowledged mastery of the art of tolling, in 1988 Canada Post invited Avery Nickerson to give an address at an important event in Nova Scotia tolling retriever history. In honour of the CKC's one hundredth anniversary, Canada Post unveiled four stamps featuring a quartet of dogs designated as true Canadian breeds. One was the little red retriever from Nova Scotia. At the stamp's unveiling in Yarmouth on August 26, 1988, Avery Nickerson gave the following speech:

"It gives me great pleasure to talk to you this afternoon about my favourite subject, the Nova Scotia Duck Tolling Retriever, particularly with this being the day that these fine little animals are being given their greatest publicity, namely the introduction of a Canadian stamp.

"There are many people in this province, across Canada and the United States who have never heard of the Toller, let alone ever seen one. However, there are many who have, particularly over the past ten to twenty years. Many of the people who have seen or heard of the Toller believe that they are a new hunting dog. Those with this assumption, through no fault of their own, are very wrong.

"I personally believe that the Toller may have been in this country as long as the French Acadians. Certainly there is no written history to substantiate their time here.

"However, fifty years ago, in discussing the dogs with an eighty-year-old French Acadian [Eddie Kenney] of Little River Harbour, Yarmouth County, I was advised that his father and grandfather had bred the Toller when he was a boy.

"The first Tollers were registered with the Canadian Kennel Club in 1945. They were owned by Col. Cyril Colwell of Halifax. In 1958 another bloodline was registered by Mrs. Hettie Bidewell of Moose Jaw, Sask., who acquired dogs from the Armstrongs of Bellneck, Yarmouth County.

"During the late 1950s, Eldon Pace of Shubenacadie and myself had bred the necessary generations and established two more bloodlines known as the Schubendorf and Green Meadows Lines. They were CKC registered in 1962. At this time only fourteen Tollers were registered with the Canadian Kennel Club. Since that time there have been a fair number of Tollers bred and offspring have found their way across the North American continent and into Europe.

"Much research has been done throughout Canada, the United States, and Europe, but nowhere are there written facts about the Toller. There have been many stories written locally as to where they originated and what dogs were utilized to make up those breeds.

"We do know, however, that they are unique because every other breed of waterfowl retriever must be kept hidden from the ducks and geese when hunting; the Toller, in contrast, is exhibited in plain view and, as a result, attracts the birds.

"Over the past fifty years, I have hunted with the Toller constantly and have witnessed hundreds of Canada Geese and, on occasion, a few thousand black ducks, raise their heads and swim swiftly and sometimes even fly directly to shore quacking and hissing at the dog that may be only a few feet from them.

"Hunters are concealed during the ritual, with an object such as a short stick, ball, or dummy to be thrown out. The dog will hastily retrieve it back to the master however many times necessary to lure the ducks within gun range. The dog is stayed and then the little red dog becomes a retriever and the [dead] birds are retrieved to the hunter . . .

"Ducks and geese react to the Toller in the same way they would to a fox. The only difference is that hunters are hidden in the blind with shotguns. It is my firm belief that birds respond to the dog because they are so similar in size, colour, agility, and performance to the fox.

"Although the standards for the Toller allow a male up to fifty pounds and a female thirty to forty pounds, most hunters prefer a smaller type more in the thirty to forty pound range for either sex.

"Tollers maintain a very friendly disposition, are especially good with children and love to participate in family activities. They are easy to train for hunting or just family pets.

"They remain very playful all their lives of twelve to sixteen years. They have very natural instincts, whether for waterfowl or upland game birds. Their undercoat is much like the down of a duck, thus withstanding cold water temperatures. They adapt well to variable temperatures from Alaska to the Gulf of Mexico.

"Having bred Tollers over the past forty years, with most of our dogs placed with waterfowl hunters, response from these people indicates their satisfaction with this little dog [and] makes breeding them all worthwhile.

Nova Scotia Duck Tolling Retriever • Retriever Duck Tolling de la Nouvelle-Écosse

The stamp was issued to celebrate the CKC's one hundredth anniversary in 1988.

"In closing, I wish to thank the people who are responsible for the decision to introduce the Nova Scotia Duck Tolling Retriever stamp in commemoration of the one hundredth anniversary of the Canadian Kennel Club.

"It certainly is felt that every Nova Scotian should be proud of this little unique dog that has been used in this area for many, many years. To quote a very prominent *Sports Afield* writer: 'the breed has every qualification to be one of the most popular sporting breeds in the United States.'

"This dog carries the name of our province and, to the best of our knowledge, originates here in Yarmouth County, N.S., Canada. Let's preserve it and be proud that it all started here in Nova Scotia."

W. Avery Nickerson passed away in April 1992; Erna, in November 1997. During their lifetimes, both Avery and Erna had worked diligently to produce the best hunting Nova Scotia Duck Tolling Retrievers possible. Toward that end, they had limited their sale of puppies mainly to hunters who would use the dogs in the traditional manner. They conscientiously avoided show ring people as buyers.

As a result, relatively few Harbourlight dogs have been recorded in the title books of the CKC. When an owner did venture onto the dog show circuit with a Harbourlight dog, however, the results were generally excellent.

One such dog was Harbourlights Roxy Watson owned by Paul Watson of Saint John, N.B. Roxy achieved her Companion Dog Title at fourteen months of age, a Companion Dog Excellent at fifteen months, passed her Working Certificate at sixteen months, and topped her achievements at twenty-three months by becoming an Obedience Trial Champion. To make Roxy's achievements even more unique, she was the first dog her owner had ever trained.

Another Harbourlight show ring notable was Harbourlights Highland Chance owned and trained by Ron MacMillan of Bathurst, N.B. The little dog from Yarmouth went High In Trial on both days of a two-day show in September 1996. She achieved her Companion Dog title in three straight shows on those days. It was Ron and Chance's first ever show ring appearance.

In spite of successes of this kind, Avery and Erna continued to resist show ring buyers. They also sold only limited breeding stock to Canadian breeders, apparently preferring to sell such dogs to European or American breeders.

Certainly, orders were always rolling in for Harbourlight puppies and there was usually a waiting list. Over the years many magazine articles have been

Harbourlights Highland Chance (September 15, 1996) won High in Trial. She's shown here with judge Betty Reid and owner Ron MacMillan. (Photo Walter Norris)

written about the Nickersons and their dogs. These stories drew many buyers their way. Harbourlights Highland Chance and her half-sister Harbourlights Scotia Ceilidh together appeared in more than twelve magazine articles about the Nickersons as well as in the international breed book *The Nova Scotia Duck Tolling Retriever* by Alison Strang and Gail MacMillan.

After adding forty years of promoting, protecting, and nurturing to the Nova Scotia Duck Tolling Retriever story, the Nickersons and their immense contribution to the development of Nova Scotia's provincial dog must take a prominent place in the history of this Maritime icon. Their remarkable dogs are the result of the longevity of love for one unique canine breed.

13

James Jeffery
Vision and Insight

In the early 1970s a man of vision and insight began an ambitious campaign on behalf of Nova Scotia's Duck Tolling Retrievers. Yarmouth born and bred James Jeffery set about having the fascinating tolling retrievers of Nova Scotia declared Canada's National Dog.

"The Nova Scotia Duck Tolling Retriever was developed in Canada by Canadians and for Canadian hunting conditions," he declared. "My objective is to have the Nova Scotia Duck Tolling Retriever recognized as Canada's National Dog, to take its rightful place in our Canadian heritage."

Born in 1938, James Jeffery was introduced to tolling retrievers at an early age. He recalls his first very own Toller was an old bitch named Butch that was given to him when he was a child by Avery Nickerson. In 1969 he acquired the first of his breeding stock and together with his brother-in-law Doug Coldwell set up a Nova Scotia Duck Tolling Retriever breeding kennel first named Jeffery Colwell, later Little River to reflect the dogs' ancestral home.

Graduated from university and married to Deanna, Doug's sister, Jim began to plan his strategy to make the Nova Scotia Duck Tolling Retriever Canada's official dog. Like Vincent Pottier before him, Jim realized publicity was the key. He too, embarked on a campaign that would bring his canines into the dog fancy spotlight.

In 1970 Jim and Deana began showing their favourite Toller, Red Russel of Jeffery. Soon, with Deanna handling the dog in the ring, Red had won his way to Top Conformation Toller for 1970.

The couple was disappointed, however, with Red's showing at Canadian Kennel Club licensed shows. Jim felt that this was largely a result of the breed's standards as laid out in 1945. He felt the modern dogs did not

Jim Jeffery with Ch. Red Russell of Jeffery, the dog that established the Little River Kennels, April 1969. (Courtesy James Jeffery)

have the weight and colouring that was set in those standards.

By the mid-1970s Jim and Deanna had moved to Ottawa leaving Doug Coldwell to operate the kennel in Nova Scotia. Ottawa, however, did put Jim nearer to home plate in his battle to have Nova Scotia Duck Tolling Retrievers named Canada's National Dog.

There he became a tireless champion of his cause. He was one of the first to promote the formation of a National Nova Scotia Duck Tolling Retriever Club and wrote numerous articles on the breed, which were published in Canada, the United States, and in Australia. Along the way, he fought for a revision of the CKC standard for the breed.

By the late 1970s, Jim, Deanna, and their children had moved to Elliot Lake. Removed from what he considered the centres of Toller activity, Jim handed over his interest in Little River Kennel to his brother-in-law and largely retired his efforts in the Canadian National Dog campaign.

He has not lost interest in Tollers, however, and his efforts did inspire others. In a January 1994 letter to Toller breeder Alison Strang of Surrey, B. C., he shared the following insights gathered during his years of association with Nova Scotia Duck Tolling Retrievers.

"In my mind, the origins of the breed no doubt rest with people like Eddie Kenney in the Little River Harbour area of Yarmouth County. What breeds were involved?…Probably any that were available. Some logical choices would have been hounds, cattle and sheep dogs and water dogs, because these are the dogs the practical people of that area would have available to them. Unlikely many, if any, were purebred. I watched

in my own lifetime as a few keen hunters in Yarmouth County developed dogs for hunting snowshoe rabbits. Some of these were black and tan type dogs, but no larger than a thirteen-inch Beagle; many were large hounds, although not as large as their probable ancestors. To some degree this is still going on, although I know both Beagle and Basset (purebred) stock has been more recently introduced. I recount this story only to demonstrate the ingenuity of the hunters of that area when it comes to fulfilling a need for a hunting dog. Fancy names like purebred don't cut it with most of these people. Does what its supposed to, good at it, etc. that's what counts.

"Early on, I recognized there were distinct types of Tollers in our Little River Kennel. One I called the Chin-Peek/Schubendorf line, the other I called the Green Meadows line. Chin-Peek was Hettie Bidewell's kennel name and their size and structure reflected the Belleville area preference for very small Tollers. Schubendorf was the kennel name of Eldon Pace from Shubenacadie, N.S. These dogs were a deep red with good matching bone structure.

"My Green Meadows line were large dogs, fifty to sixty pounds, twenty to twenty-one inches with bone structure to match. It had been my intent to try to maintain my two lines because the Toller gene pool was so small. But alas, we lost Rusty (our last of this line) in an accident.

"Green Meadows, I believe, was Avery and Erna Nickerson's early kennel name. The dogs in this line were like bulldozers, go for it no matter what. Loved to play but not as agile as the smaller dogs. These were rough dogs that could take rough handling, great for use along the coast as opposed the marshes and inland lakes. With an enthusiasm that bordered on wildness, they were

Ch. Red Russell with a mixed pile of teal and black ducks on opening day of duck season, 1970. (Courtesy James Jeffery)

nevertheless trainable and powerful natural retrievers.

"According to letters I have on file, one from a former CKC director that was involved, registrations from the Tollers originally registered in 1945 ran out, additional specimens being 'judged' and re-registered in the late 1950s, early 1960s. At the time I was trying to find out how current (1970s) dogs were related to the 1945 dogs. They apparently were not related at all. Thus the newer registered dogs had a larger Yarmouth content than I had suspected.

"By the early 1970s we had not yet achieved a very high degree of genetic homozygosity. I suppose whatever breeders had been doing was the same as Yarmouth breeders had done for one hundred years in developing the Toller.

"I assume the gene pool outside Yarmouth is now large enough not to have to worry about this kind of thing any more. I also assume Little River Duck Dogs are still being bred as they always were. I wonder what they look like today?"

Recently, Jim has wrapped up a near successful bid to become his riding's representative in the Federal Government of Canada. Still very much the crusader, Jim ran for election out of a desire to help Canada's rural population.

14

David Wood

Historian and Show Ring Pioneer

David Wood of Springhill became interested in Nova Scotia Duck Tolling Retrievers in the early 1970s. Intrigued by their nebulous history, he began to investigate their past. His inquiries led him to become one of the few Nova Scotians since Col. Cyril Colwell to delve into Toller roots and trace one important early bloodline, the Hatfield strain, to its possible conclusion. His dedication to such research would later be rewarded by several Tollers that assisted him to outstanding success in the show ring.

Born in Springhill in 1947, David has shared his interest in Nova Scotia Duck Tolling Retrievers with his wife Sheila who hails from Lunenburg County. Presently a mathematics teacher at Springhill High School, David first became acquainted with Tollers when he lived in Bridgewater.

"My first Toller [1972] was from a litter bred by Gerry Somers of Arcadia, Yarmouth County, from Nickerson stock," David recalls. "In the spring of that year, a friend told me about Gerry's pups. I had read about Tollers and had been anxious to see one for several years, so off we went.

"When we arrived, Gerry sent me out to a stall in the barn. I was a bit apprehensive about walking in on a bitch with a three-week-old litter but was assured that it wouldn't upset her.

"That proved to be an understatement. I couldn't imagine a friendlier and more relaxed mother. It was then that I decided this was the breed for me.

"My first pup (from that litter) lacked leg and colour but he was a fantastic retriever with tremendous spirit and intelligence."

By 1973, David was completely enthralled with this little dog and bought a second, a bitch, from the

Taffy, one of David Wood's dogs, looks keen and alert, ready for anything it seems. (Courtesy David Wood)

second litter at John and Mary Sproul's Springhill Kennel. After that, he became an occasional breeder and an involved historian of the little red dogs from Yarmouth.

In the course of his research, David came to think that today's Tollers could be remotely related to the fifteenth-century Royal Dog of Holland, the *Kooikerhond*. This possibility had also been investigated by Colonel Colwell. Armed with this theory, David began to explore several well-known old bloodlines in the Yarmouth area. By the mid-1970s he was deeply involved in this research.

"In 1975 I had my first look at the Armstrong line. Mr. Armstrong was a fine gentleman who gave us many interesting insights into the breed. He had several dogs that had been line-bred, to his personal knowledge, for over fifty years and that had been in the family well before that. He had had a chance to participate in the initial CKC registrations but had seen no reason to bother. He said he only sold a few dogs periodically.

"His dogs were very active and of good colour but quite small. He explained that they hunted from fixed blinds on lakes, and always had a boat for retrieving so the dogs served exclusively as Tollers. He said the bigger dogs were usually bred by those wishing to retrieve from the ocean surf."

David's attempts to trace another strain of Yarmouth tolling retriever, although in his opinion, "less rewarding," established the probable fate of another old bloodline. He was endeavouring to find the so-called "old French Toller" from which those owned by the Hatfield family of Yarmouth were supposedly descended.

Senator Paul Hatfield of Yarmouth County had made an attempt during the 1930s to have Nova Scotia's tolling retrievers recognized by the CKC. In 1966, seventy-eight-year-old Lloyd Hatfield told *Field and Stream* writer Nicholas Karas that he [Lloyd] had been among those responsible for the dogs' eventual CKC acceptance as a breed.

In the mid-1970s David's quest to find some of the last of these Hatfield dogs took him to a back street in Yarmouth. The Acadian gentleman he met there said that he hunted sea ducks from dories and did no tolling. His dogs (supposedly of the Hatfield strain) were simply tossed overboard to retrieve fallen birds.

"He showed me a bitch that was not a bad specimen and her pup," David says. "The pup looked unexplainably a little strange … until a neighbour's Beagle crawled out from under the old car in this gentleman's yard."

David's devotion to Tollers, however, would be repaid when his first obedience Nova Scotia Duck Tolling Retriever, Gypsy Lady, won a High in Trial in the late 1970s.

"A few years before, I had gone to a local obedience trainer to inquire about attending classes," David recalls. "There I was told Tollers are untrainable, that 'they are too foolish and only good for chasing sticks!'

"Later, this same person was at the dog show where Gypsy received High in Trial. I took great delight in walking past him with my rosette and prizes.

"Gypsy was always a hit at trials. Her beauty and polished performance never failed to draw a crowd."

Indeed, Gypsy finished her career as a Canadian Obedience Trial Champion.

David is an avid hunter but not of waterfowl and admits he has hunted with his Tollers only a few times. He has, however, over the past twenty years, bred champions both in conformation and obedience. Nevertheless, no matter what their titles, the Woods' dogs always remain what Nova Scotia's tolling retrievers have been for centuries, beloved family companions. This is a fact much appreciated by the Woods' two daughters, Lisa and Christine.

David believes an important aspect of any activity in which you participate is the people you meet and here he has high praise for Nova Scotia's "Toller people," especially Springhill Toller kennel owners, Mary and John Sproul.

"They are a couple whose names are synonymous with giving; in all aspects of their lives they generously share their time and resources with those around them," David says. "Mary's probably the most knowledgeable Toller person today and certainly one of the greatest contributors to the present popularity of the breed. She is willing to share her knowledge with anyone interested in learning and yet generously stands in the background and lets others claim the 'expert' title."

Mary Sproul made Nova Scotia tolling retriever history on June 1, 1980, when a dog bred at her kennel was the first Nova Scotia Duck Tolling Retriever to get a Best in Show. Mork, Sproul's Highland Playboy, owned by Linda Barnes of Regina, Sask., led the way in the show that day at Battleford, Sask.

David thoroughly enjoys his Nova Scotia Duck Tolling Retrievers and the people with whom he has

David Wood's remarkable obedience dog, Gypsy Lady. (Courtesy David Wood)

come in contact as a result of his interest in these unique little dogs. He has only one complaint.

"It's how the dogs' history is often portrayed," he says. "They have been part of this province for more than three hundred years, yet they are frequently described as being developed in the 1860s from dog breeds that they most surely predate.

"This tale was expounded by a local breeder who felt it gave the tolling retriever a story and that they were better off with this one than none at all. People such as Avery Nickerson, Col. Cyril Colwell, and Nicolas Denys, however, were confident of their being here 'as long as the Acadians.'

"I wish others would recognize their true historical significance."

15

Allister Surette

Promoting Provincial Pride

"I believe the adoption of the Nova Scotia Duck Tolling Retriever as our Provincial Dog will be a great source of pride for Nova Scotians and a living symbol of our heritage for generations to come," MLA for Argyle, Allister Surette, declared in his remarks for Second Reading of the Provincial Dog Act in May 1995. "The Nova Scotia Duck Tolling Retriever is a dog breed worthy to be the Provincial Dog of Nova Scotia. It has over three hundred years of existence in our beautiful province. The good-natured little red dog has a distinct Nova Scotian heritage of which all Nova Scotians can be proud."

The other members of the legislature agreed. On Thursday, May 11, 1995, Nova Scotia became the first Canadian Province or Territory to have an official canine. Not even Newfoundland has declared the breed that bears its name officially theirs.

Such acts, however, do not pass easily through the House. "Much time and research was needed at the onset as to the relevancy of giving the Duck Tolling Retriever the title of Provincial Canine," Mr. Surette admits. "Nevertheless, the initiative proved very interesting and a definite learning experience from the start."

It was appropriate that Allister Surette be the person to propose such legislation. A native of Lower West Pubnico, Yarmouth County, the child of a fisherman and a fish plant worker, Allister was a true son of the land of the Nova Scotia Duck Tolling Retriever. He had attended Ste-Anne-du Ruisseau High School in Yarmouth County and later received a Bachelor of Science Degree from Dalhousie University and a Bachelor of Education from St. Mary's University. He then worked as a high school teacher for nine years.

First elected to the Nova Scotia Legislature in May 1993, Allister soon became Deputy Government House Leader. In March 1995 he was appointed as government's Special Policy Advisor on Acadian and Francophone governance for the public school system.

Allister Surette was instrumental in having the Nova Scotia Duck Tolling Retriever officially recognized as Nova Scotia's provincial dog. (Courtesy Allister Surette)

On June 6, 1997, he took on a second portfolio. In September 1996, he was appointed Chairman of Team South West, a cabinet committee actively involved in economic and tourism development in south-western Nova Scotia.

Given Allister's interest both in Acadian affairs and tourism, it was natural for him to promote the Nova Scotia Duck Tolling Retriever, a product of his home area. By the 1990s the little red dog from Yarmouth was achieving international recognition as a remarkable and unique breed.

"The promotion of the Nova Scotia Duck Tolling Retriever as a symbol for Nova Scotia will enhance tourism," Allister Surette declared in his address to the legislature, which expressed his desire to have the breed officially recognized by the government. "But most of all, it can be a unifying source of pride for all Nova Scotians . . . and a living symbol of our heritage for generations to come."

In 1995 Allister began his campaign to have the Nova Scotia Duck Tolling Retriever declared Nova Scotia's provincial dog. That year marked the fiftieth anniversary of the breed's recognition as a distinct breed by the Canadian Kennel Club.

He introduced the bill as a Private Member's Bill "because of the dogs' roots in the Little River Harbour/Comeau's Hill region of Yarmouth County where it is often called the Little River Duck Dog or Yarmouth Toller."

Allister says he has always had a fondness for dogs and although he himself does not hunt or own a Toller, he has many friends who do and declare the Nova Scotia Duck Tolling Retriever to be an invaluable hunting companion. He has appeared on the television's "Midday" with a Nova Scotia Duck Tolling Retriever and its owner/breeder and says that since the breed's official recognition by the province, he has received correspondence and calls from all over Canada and the United States inquiring about the dogs.

Born in Yarmouth on September 21, 1961, Allister married Jill MacKenzie in 1984. The couple now have two young daughters, Leslie and Kate.

A man whose roots, like those of the Nova Scotia Duck Tolling Retriever, are firmly planted in south-western Nova Scotia, Allister Surette has succeeded in establishing a special niche in the province's history both for himself and the now provincial breed.

The following is an excerpt from "Assembly Debates Nova Scotia Legislature" on Thursday, May 11, 1995 regarding Bill No. 14 - Provincial Dog Act.

MR. SPEAKER: The honourable Government House Leader.

HON. RICHARD MANN: Mr. Speaker, would you please call Bill No. 14 - Provincial Dog Act

MR. ALLISTER SURETTE: Mr. Speaker, I am pleased to have the opportunity to say a few words in moving second reading of this bill. The Nova Scotia Duck Tolling Retriever has sometimes been called Nova Scotia's best kept secret and with good reason . . .

Today, there are approximately six breeders here in the province and two dozen across Canada. The Toller is also known as the Little River Duck Dog due to its place of origin, Little River Harbour, Yarmouth County, found in the constituency of Argyle.

This breed has over three hundred years of documented existence in this province. The early use of tolling dogs are recorded in fifteenth-century Holland. Later these dogs were introduced into England,

Curiosity killed the duck; a tolling retriever brings in the kill. (Courtesy Ron MacMillan)

Belgium, and France, and it may well have been their presence in France that led to their introduction in Acadia, which is now known as the Maritime Provinces.

There is documentation that states that the Toller was not at any stage of its development influenced by breedings in any other country. The Nova Scotia Duck Tolling Retriever can be called the only true Canadian Dog. It was developed here in Canada by a Canadian for Canadian hunting purposes.…

It has, Mr. Speaker, received recognition once before. To mark the one hundredth anniversary of the Canadian Kennel Club in 1988, Canada Post unveiled four new dog stamps, each bearing a truly Canadian dog, the Nova Scotia Duck Tolling Retriever being one of the dogs portrayed.

The preservation and promotion of the Nova Scotia Duck Tolling Retriever is due to the efforts of a handful of dedicated owners and breeders. Col. Cyril Colwell of Colwell Brothers of Halifax was in large part responsible for promoting the dog until his death in 1962. In 1945, Colonel Colwell succeeded in gaining national recognition for the breed [when] the Canadian Kennel Club officially recognized the Nova Scotia Duck Tolling Retriever as a distinct breed.

In Yarmouth in the early 1960s, two other breeders, Eldon Pace and Avery Nickerson devoted much of their time to developing the breed.

Mr. Speaker, on August 12, 1995, this summer, the Nova Scotia Duck Tolling Retriever Club of Canada will be holding a national specialty dog show at Cole Harbour Place. This event will commemorate the fiftieth anniversary of recognition of the retriever as a distinct breed by the Canadian Kennel Club.

In closing, I find it very appropriate to declare the Nova Scotia Duck Tolling Retriever the official provincial dog as it is a living part of our heritage. With that, Mr. Speaker, I move second reading.

The motion was carried. The result is our Provincial Dog, the Nova Scotia Duck Tolling Retriever.

Left: Tom Doucette of Ireton, Yarmouth County, cuddles a Nova Scotia Duck Tolling Retriever pup named Pete, August 1997. (Courtesy Andy Wallace)

Lower left: Zack—bred by Avery Nickerson and owned by Ralph Crowell. (Courtesy Dianne Crowell, Photo S. Crowell)

Lower right: Harbourlights Highland Chance rests after bringing in a Canada goose. (Photo Ron MacMillan)

Top: *Ralph Crowell and Zack on a hunting trip. (Courtesy Dianne Crowell)*

Lower left: *A beautiful pose is struck! (Courtesy Andy Wallace)*

Lower right: *One of today's Little River Duck Dogs enjoying a restful moment. (Courtesy Evelyn LeBlanc)*

Harbourlights Ceilidh (left) and Harbourlights Chance (right) enjoy the surf. The duck-down-like layer of fur next to their skin helps to insulate these dogs in cold water. (Courtesy Ron MacMillan)

—*16*—

Twice Told Toller Tales

The following stories have been told by Yarmouth residents acquainted with Nova Scotia's tolling retrievers for many years. Without their input, many valuable pieces of information and bits of previously unwritten history could have been missed.

Anne Boudreau

I was put in contact with Bruno Boudreau through a telephone call from his niece Anne. Anne advised me that her uncle knew a great deal about the early days of the Little River Duck Dog.

Anne herself, however, proved an excellent source of information. She described duck hunts in the Comeau's Hill area of Yarmouth County when she was a girl. She told the story of roasting ducks' feet in the ovens of wood stoves and how they would puff up and make fine eating.

Anne recalled watching duck hunters on an island off Comeau's Hill through binoculars. She remembers those hunters coming home with their Little River Dogs and bags of ducks. Some of these dogs were darker or lighter in colour than today's Nova Scotia

Duck Tolling Retrievers and some had long hair and some short. All were keen hunters.

To illustrate this fact, Anne told the story of one of her grandfather's Little River Dogs actually bursting through a window when he discovered the shotgun missing from behind the door. He thought his master had gone hunting without him.

Bruno Boudreau

After speaking with Anne, I was anxious to talk to her uncle and called him the next evening. Bruno Boudreau of Little River Harbour and his father before him have always owned Little River Duck Dogs. He recalls his Uncle Henry Boudreau coming to his home one night just as it was getting dark and saying he'd shot two ducks but had been unable to get them. He

Gerald Boudreau of Little River Harbour clutches two Little River pups, circa 1930s. (Courtesy Yarmouth County Museum and Archives)

took Bruno's dog and went back out. There was ice and other ducks quacking in the darkness. Undaunted, the little dog retrieved both ducks.

Bruno told me his dogs sometimes did a double retrieve; that is, bringing two ducks in at once, gripped by a neck or a wing or some combination thereof. He recalls his dogs diving after bluebills and whistlers, two species of diving ducks, in the process of retrieving them.

Bruno knew Eddie Kenney of Comeau's Hill/Little River Harbour and regards him as the true founder of the Little River Duck Dog breed. He's skeptical about the half fox theory. He believes Eddie Kenney drew on good duck tolling retriever dogs of all types to develop his dogs.

Bruno describes the tolling retriever as being about the size of a red fox, red in colour, with white on the chest, face, and tips of feet and tail. Now seventy-five years of age, Bruno concluded our conversation with a simple yet complete description of the dogs.

"They're just wonderful," he said.

Adolphe (Dossie) Fitzgerald

Adolphe (Dossie) Fitzgerald of Little River Harbour was, like Eddie Kenney, an influential breeder and trainer of tolling retrievers during the first half of the twentieth century. More importantly, however, it is believed Dossie was the first Yarmouth County breeder to ship pups abroad to France and England prior to World War II.

Evelyn LeBlanc, Dossie's cousin (Dossie's father William was her uncle) says Dossie's great-grandfather John came to the Comeau's Hill area of Yarmouth County from Ireland following the Napoleanic Wars. A second John Fitzgerald was Dossie's grandfather.

Dossie was born on January 27, 1881. He married three times: in 1901 Jessie Muise; in 1922 Elizabeth Fitzgerald, a widow; and in 1939 Agnes Kenny. He died in 1960.

"He guided many famous people," Evelyn LeBlanc recalls. "We didn't take note of who they were at the time, though."

It is believed that some of these celebrity clients carried word of Dossie's remarkable tolling retrievers abroad. This apparently resulted in orders for puppies from the United States and parts of Europe.

Sam Rodgerson

Sam Rodgerson of Melbourne Road, Yarmouth County, wrote to me after seeing a letter to the editor which I had placed in *The Yarmouth Vanguard* requesting information on Nova Scotia's tolling retrievers. I was delighted to discover Sam Rodgerson, at age eighty-seven, is an ardent admirer of the breed, a wealth of information on the subject, and a distinct pleasure to interview.

Sam remembers Eddie Kenney of Comeau's Hill/Little River Harbour as the man who first established Yarmouth's tolling retrievers as a distinct breed. He knew Eddie well. Sam first met him when he (Sam) was a teenager and recalls Eddie, a fisherman by profession, raising the dogs.

"He sold them, I would guess, for about five dollars," he says. "But then, you have to remember, five dollars was a fair amount in those days.

"Eddie had a small breeding stock. Probably only a couple of bitches and a male."

Sam Rodgerson's affection and admiration for these Little River Duck Dogs shine in his every word.

Although he did not own one until after he retired, he recalls fifty years with many exciting days of ducking with the tolling retrievers of friends by his side. He remembers seeing ducks coming so close to the dog they would spit on him.

"I especially remember one day when friends and I went up to Gemseg Bay in New Brunswick. Looking across a field, we spotted a huge flock of black ducks rafting peacefully far out on the water.

"We went to the farmer who owned the field and asked him if he would allow us to cross it and hunt the ducks. He agreed but warned, 'You'll never get them to come any closer.'

"We made our way across the field and hid in the grass beside the water. Then we set Queenie, one of our tolling retrievers, to work.

"Within a few minutes, many [ducks] were moving toward shore. What an incredible sight!

"We got our limit and left a pair at the farmer's door on our way out. He wasn't home. I wish he had been. I would have liked to know if he saw those ducks, so impossible to bring in, heading for shore like iron filings to a magnet."

These days Sam owns his own tolling retriever that he affectionately refers to as his ears. She is always ready to tell him when someone is at the door. For Sam, a lifetime of admiration for the little red dogs of Yarmouth County is being repaid with the companionship and devotion of one among their number.

Evelyn LeBlanc

On September 1, 1997, I received a most enjoyable letter from eighty-three-year-old Evelyn LeBlanc of West Pubnico, Yarmouth County. A cousin of Adolphe (Dossie) Fitzgerald, she told her story in a way that is best recounted as she wrote it.

"I am a lady of eighty-three years and well remember the Little River Duck Retrievers. One of my cousins, Adolphe Fitzgerald known as Dossie, trained these dogs for Paul Trask of Yarmouth. I remember him [Dossie] talking to these dogs as if they were human.

"During duck hunting time, both dog and hunter were well alert to what was going on. Dossie would say to his dog, 'Gunner, we are going duck hunting. Get my boots, my jacket, and my gun.' Up Gunner would jump and get every one of the articles Dossie had named. Then off they would go. When they came back, they would have every duck they had killed.

"When rabbit hunting time came along, off they would go to the woods. When Dossie would say, 'Quiet' the dog would stand still, then when the hunter would crawl on his belly, the dog would also.

"These dogs were sold for as much as $150 . . . that was big money then. After Dossie, Bruno and Henry Boudreau trained these dogs for years. All these men lived in Little River Harbour.

"I grew up, got married and had children. I was given a dog trained by Gordon Cann. Mine was trained as a house pet and guardian. When I went out with my twin babies, my dog would follow me. Every time I would stop, the dog would sit by the carriage and no one would touch it until I would come out.

"When I was alone at night, he would be right at my feet until my husband came home. Then he felt we were safe.

"I had him for five years. Then the distemper virus was in Yarmouth and he got sick. We had to make away with him. To my sorrow."

John Jeffery

On July 3, 1978, Jim Jeffery interviewed eighty-four-year-old John Jeffery of East Kentville, Yarmouth County, a long-time tolling retriever user. John recalled he had gotten his first tolling retriever many years before from a man named Brindley of Comeau's Hill.

A few years later a local man accused his neighbours' dogs of worrying his sheep and drove through the community throwing poison in every yard. John's dog died as a result of this random destruction even though John knew the animal was innocent. He said people in Yarmouth County had, for years, used tolling retrievers for herding. These dogs were not sheep worriers.

John declared he had gotten some of this best dogs in the Comeau's Hill/Little River Harbour area. His last tolling retriever (in the 1970s) he described as a "great dog." He said that dog had often led him to his blind when he himself got a little confused. His love and respect for his tolling retrievers over many years were obvious in every word.

Canny and Courageous Canines

Nova Scotia's tolling retrievers over the years have shown a bravery and wisdom that has made their owners rate them among their most trusted companions. Dianne Crowell related the following incidents involving one of her father's favourite dogs.

"One of Dad's dogs, Trixie, once saved my life. She was keeping me company at my farmhouse one night when a log in the fireplace rolled forward and, because of an unusual amount of pitch, began smoking up the whole house.

"Trixie would never get on the bed, but that night she jumped up and sat on my chest in an effort to wake me. We both had to crawl through the house to the door and out onto the lawn. I'm sure I would have died of smoke inhalation if not for Trixie's persistence.

"Later, when Trixie's pal Trevor, Dad's other Little River at the time, got caught in a trap, Trixie ran to my Aunt Hazel's house and sounded the alarm by barking and refusing to come in and visit. Hazel's husband Eddie immediately suspected something was seriously wrong; Trixie was usually a quiet and friendly dog.

"He followed her through the woods, found Trevor, and released him from the trap. Fortunately Trevor had suffered only a minor injury.

"Of all the Little Rivers my father had, I believe Trixie was his favourite. His eyes still tear up when he tells stories of their adventures."

Toller Tales that Tickle

In the many conversations with tolling retriever people involved with compiling this manuscript, some of my most enjoyable moments came with the telling of jokes and (possibly) tall tales. They are a fitting footnote to the story of these wonderful people.

Of course, being frank and down-to-earth individuals, they did admit there could be the occasional "poor" tolling retriever but never a bad one. Their love and admiration for their little dogs would not allow them to use so harsh a description.

One of the most amusing tales about one of these "poor" tolling retrievers was one told by a hunter with more than fifty years of experience with the dogs. When he was asked exactly what was wrong with the dog, he said the animal was too slow.

"You could throw a stick for him to fetch and eat your lunch before he got back," he explained. "I finally gave him to my neighbour who wanted a house pet. The dog was good at that job."

Certainly stories of good tolling retrievers dominated. One long-time duck hunter could not praise his old dog enough. She was excellent in every way even though she was not especially pretty.

"She was as broad as she was long," he said. "At a distance you couldn't tell if she was front or side on. But, could she hunt!"

Another told of once owning a tolling retriever possessed of a free-wheeling spirit; so free, in fact, the only way he could be certain of having the dog come to him was to trick him into thinking they were about to go hunting. He did this by going out into his yard and firing his shotgun into the air. Instantly his roving dog would be by his side.

There were also tips on easy tolling methods for hunters disinclined to spend a lot of time training their dogs. For example, instead of honing the dog's retrieving skills, simply tie a piece of meat to a string and throw it out of the blind when ducks are within sight. The dog will dash after it. Then, just before he grabs it, flip it back into the blind. Repeat as required. And *voilà,* a successful toll.

A couple of the tales seemed a little "tall": one about the tolling retriever who once retrieved a deer his master had shot in a lake; another about one of the little red dogs that actually tolled a moose into his master's camera range.

Then there is the story of the outlaw tolling retriever (who will go by the alias of Robin Hood in this account) who helped her master elude the law one bitter January night many years ago.

"We left home long after dark on a moonlit night," her owner recalled. "It was real cold and every once in a while it would cloud up and spit snow. We had just shot a few blacks [ducks] in a small creek on the ice when Robin Hood started growling and climbed up onto my lap. Someone was coming!

"I put her inside my white parka and covered her up.

"In a few moments, I discovered why Robin had been so upset. Game wardens! They came so close to us we could recognize them easily.

"When the coast was clear, Robin got a lot of praise. She'd saved our hides that night!"

As far as the best "toll" of ducks, one old-timer topped them all when he told of his dog tolling a flock of eleven ducks to within gun range. He managed to shoot them all. But his dog did still better. He retrieved an even dozen.

Humour was tinged with apprehension on occasion when several old-time hunters and breeders discussed their dogs' present and future.

"Most breeders these days are women," one commented. "The dogs aren't used for hunting or being bred to hunt. Because they're nice looking and smart, show rings are getting a lot of them, too."

Then, in typical "breed apart" style he lightened the mood with this anecdote. There once was a lady who knew nothing about tolling retrievers but managed to purchase one from a Yarmouth breeder. She was advised to start each toll with a quack.

Shortly, exasperated, she returned the dog to the man in disgust. When asked what the problem was, she replied angrily, "I put him out on the shore and waited and waited. But he never uttered a single quack!"

Andy Wallace
"Down in Yarmouth County"

Andy Wallace once risked his life to save his beloved tolling retriever Blu from drowning. No one can offer higher evidence of devotion and respect. A man who is the living personification of this book's theme, Andy Wallace shares an appreciation of Nova Scotia's unique little dogs equal to that of Eddie Kenney.

"Andy's dogs look a lot like my grandfather's," Audrey Goudey, Eddie's granddaughter, commented. "And Andy certainly loves them, too!"

Born in Yarmouth County in 1942, William Andrew Wallace married Phyllis Muise from Surettes Island in 1964. The couple have four children: Lisa, Mark, Todd, and Sarah. A plumber by trade, Andy was an instructor at the Community College for the past twenty-seven years until his retirement in 1997. A part-time farmer for twenty years, Andy is now free to devote his time to this avocation, his family, and his dogs.

Andy's knowledge of tolling retrievers stretches back to the days when his mother worked for V. J. Pottier. He says Judge Pottier bred two types of tolling dogs, a long-haired and a short-haired variety. He thinks there was probably close bloodline connections among many of the Belleville area tolling retrievers in those days. These would have included the Pottier, Babine, and Armstrong strains. Another probably existed among the dogs from the Comeau's Hill/Little River Harbour area.

"I owned my first Toller when I was ten or eleven," Andy recalls. "She never hunted but she did my paper route with me every day.

"I began breeding the dogs in 1968. My first brood bitch was Lady, a dog I purchased in 1965. She came from Wedgeport, Yarmouth County, her father from Comeau's Hill near Little River Harbour. Lady was bred to a dog from Tusket Falls . . . I believe he had originally been an Armstrong dog. I kept Blu from that first litter.

Andy Wallace (left) shown here with Dan and his dogs Penny and Taffy after a successful black duck hunt. (Courtesy Andy Wallace)

She and I would later share the adventure of a lifetime.

"But it was with Lady that I shared the most memorable tolling experience of my life. It happened one stormy day in December 1967. We went to one of the Tusket Islands in a lobster fishing boat. There was a strong north-east wind blowing and it was raining cats and dogs. We had to anchor the boat on the windward side of Wilson's Island and row ashore in a double end skiff, two men with the oars and one bailing steady with a five-gallon can, it was so rough.

"Finally we got to shore, drained the water from our guns, and loaded up. When we crawled over the sea wall, we could hardly believe our eyes . . . hundreds of black ducks heading for a grassy shore a couple of hundred yards away. Bringing them in was a red fox!

"He was running back and forth on the shore in the same way our tolling dogs do and when the ducks got near enough, he would jump at them, causing the ones in close to fly up fifteen or twenty feet, then land down again just out of reach.

"After four or five tries, he caught one and came back along the sea wall where we were hiding with the duck in his mouth. We were elated! We had just seen proof of the origins of tolling!

"We quickly ran down and hid in the grass where the fox had been tolling and waited. After a short while, a few blacks returned, then more and more. There were probably two hundred when I first showed Lady.

"They were immediately interested and began to swim in real fast. We shot our share and Lady retrieved every one, sometimes bringing in two birds at a time.

"As Lady brought in the last bird, we saw the flock land right back where they had been and once again begin to follow the dog back to shore. It only took a

few tosses of the stick to bring them in range again and the process was repeated.

"By then it was getting late, the tide was turning, and it was time to go. We loaded the skiff, set one man on the oars, and shoved off into the wild surf. We got swamped almost immediately, had to bail out the skiff, pick up our ducks, and start over again.

"We made it through the surf this time but even oil clothes didn't keep us dry. The guy bailing sure had a tough job with his face in the wind. Fortunately the anchor had held on the lobster boat and we were soon able to be on our way home.

"And although Lady who had shared this adventure with me was a great dog, it was her daughter Blu who became my favourite. Blu and I were to share an experience no dog and master could ever forget. It began one day in 1970.

"Blu and I were hunting alone over eel grass decoys on the mud flats. Finally a lone black duck headed in to our decoys and I shot it. It fell on the ice a long way out. I sent Blu to retrieve it but just as she picked up the bird, she broke through the ice.

"After she had struggled to get out of the water for four or five minutes, it became obvious she wasn't going to make it. I couldn't leave her to drown or freeze . . . I didn't know which would come first.

"There was only one thing I could do for her now. I raised my shotgun to my shoulder, pushed off the safety, and put my fingers on both triggers. I tried to aim but was blinded by my tears. Blu had started to cry like a baby.

"Then I remembered an old tree I had seen a few days before up on the beach. I ran up the shore, found it, pulled it free from the ice, and headed out over the channel towards Blu.

Andy de-worms Sadie's young litter, August 1997. (Courtesy Andy Wallace)

"Suddenly the ice broke under me and I went in. What relief to discover that, at that point, I was only up to my armpits!

"I broke the ice so Blu could swim to me (she was still carrying the duck). When we got near solid ice, I threw her up onto it and used the tree to get myself up and out of the water.

"The three-mile walk home that followed left both of us nearly frozen stiff. Nevertheless, we were grateful to be alive."

Andy has never regretted this kind of devotion to his Little River Duck Dogs. Show rings and titles don't mean much to him but canines like Lady, Blu, Penny, Taffy, and Sadie have found eternal places in his heart. Andy is one of those Yarmouth natives who is, as Bill McClure so aptly describes, "a living breed pioneer, a hunter for whom guns, cartridges, coats, boots, ducking, and Tollers have meant more than words can convey."

Epilogue
The Toller's Future

"Down in Yarmouth, a living breed pioneer, a hunter for whom guns, cartridges, coats, boots, ducking, and Tollers have meant more than words can convey, looks out his front window on the windswept, foggy, and ruggedly beautiful southern tip of Nova Scotia. . . . For a man who watched one of his dogs haul to shore several eel grass fat Canadas last autumn, the thought of a Toller who hasn't worked a bird is almost more than he can bear. He is right, you know."

Bill McClure *Gun Dog Magazine*, November-December 1986

One writer recently called the Toller a dead breed, a former hunting dog that today has been reduced to being a cute little pet. Another called tolling a clever trick of no real significance.

They are both wrong. Tollers as hunting companions are spreading across North America, Europe, and even Australia and New Zealand at an amazing rate. As the smallest retriever breed, these little dogs are admirably suited to the crowded lifestyle of the new millenium.

Perhaps the greatest threat to the Toller's identity lies in their intelligence and versatility. Proving to be fine show dogs, excellent agility and fly ball competitors, capable of mountain rescue work, drug detection, and tracking, as well as being fine therapy dogs, the little red canines often find themselves employed at jobs for which they were never originally intended.

While it is unrealistic to believe tolling for ducks by hunters will stay the same as it has in the past, it is a fact that these days more outdoor enthusiasts are shooting wildlife with cameras. There is no better photographic waterfowl lure than a Nova Scotia Duck Tolling Retriever; just ask my husband and photographer, Ron.

Perhaps Colonel Colwell's wish that dogs be used simply for this quiet pursuit will someday become a reality.

Harbourlights Scotia Ceilidh enjoys the shore. (Photo Ron MacMillan)

Bibliography

Adams, Charles. "Canadian Panorama. The Dog that Lures Ducks To Their Doom." *Star Weekly.* Toronto, November 27, 1971.

Admiral Digby Museum. Files. Digby, Nova Scotia, 1997. Assembly Debates.

Nova Scotia Legislature. Halifax, Thursday, May 11, 1997.

Bower, Augustus. "The Evolution of the Tolling Dog." *Rod And Gun* and *Canadian Silver Fox News.* Toronto, March 1932.

Canadian Kennel Club. Files. Stud Book 1950–1960. Breed Standards. Ontario,1960.

Canadian Press. "Senator Hatfield Passes away in Nova Scotia."

Montreal Gazette. Montreal, January 29, 1935.

Coleman, Edwin. "The Dog that Tolls." *Rod and Gun in Canada.* Toronto, March 1966.

Colwell, Col. Cyril. Files, 1923–1960. Courtesy of the Colwell Family. Halifax.

Crowell, Peter. "That Incredible 'Titan': Louis F. Babine, Professional Building Mover of Yarmouth County, 1898 - 1938."

Nova Scotia Historical Review. Vol. 9, Number 2, 1989.

Denys, Nicolas. *Description and Natural History of Coasts of North America, Acadia.* Paris. 1688. (Translation: Ganong, Prof. William F. The Champlain Society, 1908.)

Ford, Karen; MacLean, Janet; Wansbrough, Barry. *Great Canadian Lives: Portraits in Heroism to 1867.* Scarborough: Nelson, Canada, 1985.

Halpin, David J., ed. *Debates of the Senate of the Dominion of Canada.* Ottawa: J. O. Patenaude, 1935.

Jeffery, James C. Taped interviews with various tolling retriever experts. Yarmouth County, Nova Scotia, 1978.

Ch. Red Russel of Jeffery tolling ducks, Lake Milo, 1971. (Courtesy James Jeffery)

Johnson, J. K. *The Canadian Directory of Parliament, 1867–1967*. Ottawa: Public Archives of Canada. 1968.

Karas, Nicholas. "Dogs that Decoy Ducks." *Field & Stream*. New York, September, 1966.

Leaders of Nova Scotia, 1936. Yarmouth: Loyalist Press, 1936.

Les Familles du Bas-de-Tousquet (Wedgeport) 1767 à 1900. Wedgeport: Les Editions Lescarbot.

McClure, William. *Gun Dog Magazine*. DesMoines, Illinois. November-December, 1986.

Morgan, John. "Shubenacadie Wildlife Pioneer. " *Ducks Unlimited* (magazine). Saskatchewan, 1984.

Nickerson, W. Avery. Address given on unveiling of NSDTR Stamp In Yarmouth, Nova Scotia. August 26, 1988.

Normandin, A. L. (Major). *The Canadian Parliamentary Guide*. Ottawa, 1927.

Normandin. A. A. (Major). *The Canadian Parliamentary Guide*. Ottawa, 1936.

Normandin, Pierre G. *The Canadian Parliamentary Guide*. Ottawa, 1965.

Robinson, Berton, ed. *Nova Scotia, Three Hundred Years in Education*. A Centennial Project of the Nova Scotia Teachers Union.

Semple, Joan. Taped interviews for Yarmouth Museum with various tolling retriever experts. Yarmouth County, 1994.

Simpson, Kieran, ed. *Canadian Who's Who, 1979*. Toronto: University of Toronto Press, 1979.

Stamp, Robert M. *The Canadian Obituary Record*. Toronto: Dundurn Press,1990.

Smith, Stan. "The Dogs that Decoy Ducks," *Saga Magazine*. New York, November 1954.

Sutherland, William. "A Legend in his Own Pond," *Outdoor Atlantic Magazine*. November 1979.

Sutherland, William. "Nova Scotia's Tolling Dog. " *Bluenose Magazine*. Fall 1979.

The Canadian Who's Who. Vol. VIII, 1958–1960. Toronto: Trans-Canada Press, 1960.

The Chronicle-Herald. Halifax, Saturday, July 27, 1974.

The Chronicle-Herald. Halifax, Wednesday, February 4, 1980.

The Chronicle-Herald. Halifax, November 3, 1990.

Time Magazine. December 3, 1951.

Yarmouth Herald. Article entitled "Senator Paul Hatfield Dies." Yarmouth, January, 29, 1935.

Left: Harbourlights Highland Chance (back) and Harbourlights Scotia Ceilidh (fore). (Photo Ron MacMillan)

Below: An acrylic painting by William Crowell of Rusty, one of the dogs originally registered with the CKC, owned by William Sutherland of Lockeport, N.S. (Courtesy William Crowell)

Overleaf: Harbourlights Scotia Ceilidh enjoys a frolic in the snow. (Photo Ron MacMillan)